Petoskey
thirty-nine

WALKABOUTS

by
Gary W. Barfknecht

Friede Publications

39 PETOSKEY WALKABOUTS

Copyright, 2001, by Gary W. Barfknecht

*This book may not be reproduced in whole or part
by mimeograph or any other means without permission.*

Friede Publications
P.O. Box 217
Davison, Michigan 48423

514 Waukazoo Avenue
Petoskey, Michigan 49770

Printed in the United States of America

First Printing, June, 2001

ISBN 0-923756-22-1

OTHER BOOKS BY GARY W. BARFKNECHT

The Michigan Book of Bests
Unexplained Michigan Mysteries
Ultimate Michigan Adventures
Mich-Again's Day
Michillaneous (out of print)
Michillaneous II (out of print)
Murder, Michigan (out of print)

FOREWORD

When we became year-round residents of Petoskey in 1999, for recreation and exercise and to familiarize myself with my new home, I set out on a mapped and scheduled 2- to 4-mile-a-day program to walk all of the city's streets.

While doing so, I also discovered and explored many trails that led into and through woods; ran beside lakes, rivers and creeks; and afforded close encounters with and beautiful perspectives of the bay.

I'm not sure how far into my program I was when I decided to share my discoveries, observations and experiences. It was a gradual realization, not an overwhelming epiphany. I've made my living as an author and publisher of Michigan books for more than 25 years. I've been a serious walker a lot longer. This book was conceived and born from the natural union of those loves, rather than being issued from a calculated plan.

It didn't take long to do a first-time walk of all of the routes in this book. But while and after I did, I realized how much more than where to move my feet I needed to learn before I could accurately, authoritatively, and interestingly describe the paths to others. I read and reread geology textbooks plus every area history book available at bookstores and the library. I carefully examined topographical maps. And I spent countless frustrating hours fondling leaves, staring at bark, and paging through bible-thick tree-identification books while resurrecting dormant skills I had learned as a Boy Scout some 45 years ago.

To reassure myself that I had been prop-

erly self-educated and to plug some research holes, I peppered indulgent, helpful staff at city and township halls, Bay View, the state park, the public library, Little Traverse Conservancy, and other offices with questions. And I had long, especially rewarding talks with Candace Eaton, Executive Director of the Little Traverse Historical Society, and Dr. Alan Arbogast, Assistant Professor of Geology at Michigan State University.

But mostly I walked ... and walked ... and walked some more. Over two years, I walked each of the routes in this book a minimum of four — usually more — times, dictating observations and pedometer-measured distances into a microcassette recorder.

When I then composed the descriptions, I did something that goes against my writing instinct and, at first consideration, even against the principles of good guidebook writing. I determined that I would not insert value judgments; I would not offer my opinion on what was good, bad or indifferent about what I observed and experienced. Rather, I would present only neutral "facts and nothing but the facts."

Here's why. Take swamps, for instance ... please. I don't like slogging around in swamps, especially mosquito-infested swamps. Swamps don't appeal to me, even though some have tried making them sound more attractive by calling them wetlands. To me, they're damp, dank, dark, forbidding, even foreboding, and I'm therefore tempted to not-so-subtly steer others away. But there are those who like swamps — er, wetlands — and for good reasons. Wetlands are fascinating, environmentally valuable and diverse ecosystems worthy of experiencing close up.

I also have an aversion to long, straight, dead-level stretches of trail, such as along abandoned railroad beds. They drive me crazy; I feel like I'm on a treadmill with a repeating video of the same aspens moving by on each side. But to many solitary walkers, straight stretches like those are great places to lose themselves in free thought without risking literally getting lost. And groups find the same areas good places to walk briskly and hold conversations without feeling that someone is being rushed past or distracted from the scenery.

I don't even issue disclaimers or warnings about sections of routes that (usually briefly) follow busy roads or highways. I prefer off-road tranquility. But there just may be a walker who hears musical scales when a double-tandem gravel hauler shifts through 16 gears, and others who hear a chorus when a convoy of fully loaded cement trucks cruises by.

Also the ever-changing nature of the trails themselves make a complete evaluation impossible. No matter how many times any of us take any of the walks in this book, we'll never have the same experience twice. All of the walks continually change character — sometimes dramatically — especially with changes of seasons, each with its own balance of potential pluses and minuses for walkers.

In spring, for instance, the air is uniquely fresh and bug free and views are unob-structed — you can see naked topographical features like at no other time of year. But trails are often wet and muddy and colorful wildflowers and lush foliage is absent.

In summer, heavy vegetation growth cools and shades trails and hides signs of civilization, but the same greenery also can limit desirable views. Also those months are dense with tourists and seasonal-residents, and popular routes are heavily used. Lots of company is a plus to some, a turnoff to others.

After fall leaf drop, vistas expand and horizons literally broaden. However, thick leaf layers can hide toe-stubbing roots and rocks and even the trails themselves.

So to each his own. I've tried hard to remain neutral and let you sort out your own likes and dislikes. But please do the sorting. Whether you're here for a day, a weekend, a season, or a lifetime, please use this book to set up your own Discover Petoskey program. Walking is a deliciously slow, yet highly efficient way to become intimate with one of the world's most beautifully interesting areas.

Gary W. Barfknecht

A FEW RANDOM, USEFUL NOTES

• Though this is a guide written specifically for recreational walkers, many of the described routes can be and are also variously used by bicyclists, in-line skaters, people in wheelchairs, and runners. And in the winter, most trails rate good to excellent for cross-country skiing and snowshoeing, although parking areas may not be plowed and restroom and other facilities may be closed.

• Dogs are allowed on many trails but must be leashed.

• Facilities at public parks are usually open only during daylight hours in season (spring through fall).

• When walking along roads or streets with no sidewalks, stay on the left shoulder facing traffic.

• Distances — though measured several times by several methods — should be considered approximate.

• The "Allow" times are estimates that factor in a leisurely pace, with plenty of stops for long looks at what, along most routes, are remarkable views.

ON BEHALF OF ALL PETOSKEY WALKERS
THANKS TO

City and township governments, the Little Traverse Conservancy, Bay View Association, North Central Michigan College, the Michigan DNR, Top of Michigan Trails Council, service clubs, and other groups and individuals who have worked and continue to work to secure land, develop, and maintain Petoskey-area walkways.

All photos are by the author

CONTENTS

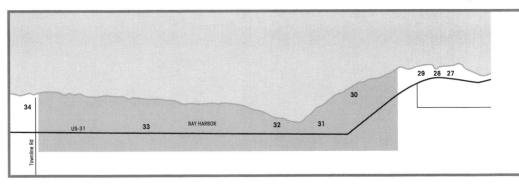

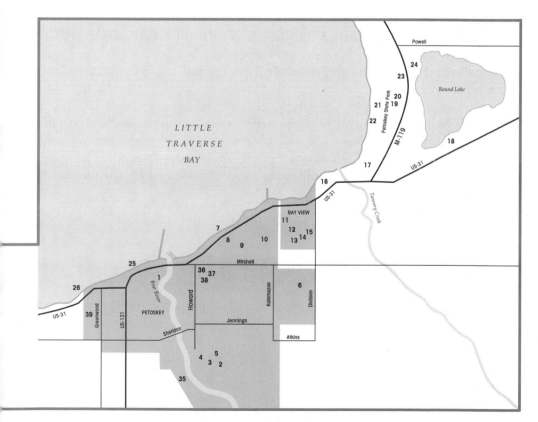

VIEWS OF THE BAY

The uniquely beautiful natural features of the Little Traverse Bay area are the result of tropical floods followed by a long, deep freeze and subsequent thaw.

Six hundred million years ago, this area was a small section of a slightly sunken, Midwest-large basin that, over the next 370 million years, intermittently filled with warm ocean water. The clear, shallow salt water teemed with marine life, including extensive coral reefs. A gradual uplifting of the earth's crust here caused the last of the vast seas to simultaneously drain away and evaporate, leaving thick beds of what became limestone, shale, dolomite, and other fossil-filled rocks.

For the next 30 million years, rivers that cut through the region carried away large areas of softer deposits, creating valleys that were the beginnings of the Great Lakes basins.

Then came the Big Chill, a 500,000- to 2-million-year-long Ice Age, when four massive ice sheets successively covered then retreated from more than a third of the earth's land surface. As the mile-thick ice flows gouged through the Midwest, they expanded the river valleys, plus the glaciers' tremendous weight depressed the valley bottoms deeper into the earth's semi-molten magma.

As the last of the glaciers receded, beginning some 14,000 years ago, meltwater filled the now-huge basins, creating a series of pre-Great lakes whose levels — for a variety of geological reasons — rose and fell several times before stabilizing at their current level about 2,500 years ago.

And the last of the great glaciers also shaped the surrounding land. As the final ice sheet moved into this area, it carried millions of tons of boulders, pebbles, sand, clay, and other pieces of the earth it had scraped, stripped, gouged and plucked from Canada. As the frozen earth mover melted and retreated, it dumped, spread and sculpted its earthen cargo into the high, rolling hills that wrap and cradle the bay, leaving a setting like no other in the world.

THE BAY

Thumb-shaped Little Traverse Bay is nine miles long, extending west from its tip at Petoskey State Park to open into Lake Michigan at an imaginary line from Bay Shore north to roughly Seven Mile Point. There it is also its widest — nearly 7 miles.

The bay is also deep, reaching down more than 190 feet near its geographic center. The irregular bottom — including a perpendicular trio of ¾-mile-long underwater ridges — is composed mostly of the limestone remains of the prehistoric saltwater oceans. Portions of the limestone contain petrified coral, pieces of which regularly break off and wash ashore as thumbnail- to boulder-size Petoskey stones, Michigan's official state rock. The 350-million-year-old fossil's characteristic gray-green, white-bordered hexagonal markings can best be seen when wet or polished.

SEVEN MILE POINT

This land that appears to jut out into the water as a sharp point actually arcs smoothly 180 degrees over 30 miles from Harbor Springs to Sturgeon Bay, north of Cross Village. The point's profile features a distinct, broad terrace that steps up from the water. About 4,000 years ago, incessant waves from a pre-Great Lake named Nipissing, which was about 25 feet higher than the current water level, gradually cut the cliff and created the large terrace below it. Though not easy to see, the terrace and bluff continue east around the bay almost to the state park.

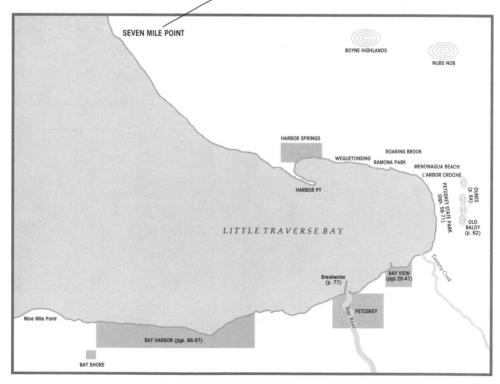

Harbor Point

Also not easy to see from water level is this narrow finger of land, which pokes a mile into the bay to help form one of Lake Michigan's finest natural harbors. Lining the point's shore are a collection of summer homes — built by old-money names such as Wrigley, Ford, Reynolds (aluminum) and Gamble (as in Proctor &) — that make up one of the Midwest's most-exclusive, gated resorts. Perched at the finger's sandy tip is the historic Little Traverse Lighthouse, which for nearly 22 years was tended by the only female lighthouse keeper on the Great Lakes.

Harbor Springs

Stepping up from the water on terraces and bluffs sculpted by prehistoric Great Lakes is the staid, upscale, turn-of-the-century resort town of Harbor Springs, known locally simply as "Harbor." What appears to be a grouping of large, white sails at the water's edge are the roofs of a condominium complex near the town's marina. A fleet of 16 real sailboats that zigzag in unison over the bay in and out of Harbor's harbor daily during the summer are skippered by sailing school students.

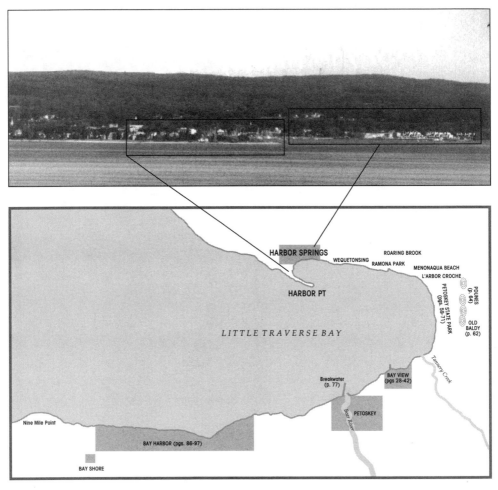

Circling the shore east from Harbor to Petoskey State Park is a series of seasonal and year-round neighborhoods and associations: Wequetonsing (known locally as "Weekwee"), Roaring Brook, Ramona Park, Menonaqua Beach, and L'Arbor Croche. Because of careful development and/or several decades worth of tree and other vegetation growth, the hundreds of homes, condos, and common facilities that make up these communities blend with or are hidden by their natural surroundings and so from across the bay are difficult to distinguish.

Interspersed with the developments are several undeveloped nature preserves owned and protected by the non-profit Little Traverse Conservancy.

Backing the bay here are the two largest of the many mounds of glacial debris — called moraines — that surround the bay, and both are noticeably marked with ski runs and designer-golf-course fairways. The 1,330-foot-above-sea-level (750 feet above the bay) mountain farthest west is home to 3,500-acre Boyne Highlands golf and ski resort. Two miles east, 41 runs of Nub's Nob ski resort drop down an equally high moraine. Some 10,000 years ago when one of the prehistoric great lakes flooded this area to a level some 160 feet higher than present, these two mountains formed a large island that poked out of the water.

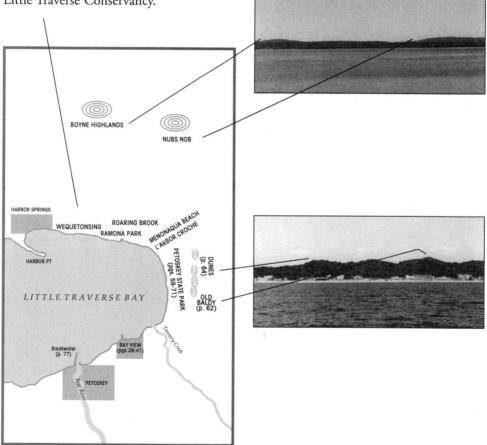

BEAR RIVER VALLEY RECREATION AREA

*Though rarely more than a few blocks from city streets, this strip-park that showcases the Bear River's final, dramatic plunge to the bay is rated by many as **the** most beautiful of greater Petoskey's many natural areas. After flowing placidly 12 miles through forest, farmland and swamps, the river drops 75 feet over its last mile, the steepest such plunge of any Lower Peninsula stream. During the past couple of thousand years, the river here has cut deeply into its limestone bed, leaving high, steep-sided banks covered with a wide variety of trees, shrubs, grasses and wildflowers. And if you come at the right time, you may spot otter, beaver, mink, songbirds, waterfowl and other wildlife.*

Around a century ago this same stretch was the simultaneous site of five dams, factories and mills that provided the city with electricity, flour, paper and lumber. During the 1960s, volunteers cleared away most of the debris left by those industries, added flood- and erosion-control rip-rap, then allowed the river to run its course.

LOOP TRAIL WITH ROUND TRIP TO SHERIDAN RD. BRIDGE, 2.3 MILES

ALLOW 1½ HOURS

LOOP TRAIL WITHOUT ROUND TRIP TO SHERIDAN RD. BRIDGE, 1.0 MILE.

ALLOW 1 HOUR

Facilities: Water fountain and picnic tables at Mineral Well Park. Restrooms behind the police/fire department building, on Lake St. on the west bank; access from outside only. Rest benches on the grassy fields on the west bank.

Directions: From the junction of US-31 and US-131, drive north then east on north US-31 0.7 miles to a traffic signal at Lake Street (the second signal after crossing the Mitchell Street Bridge and curving left, north). Or from the junction of M-119 and US-31, drive west on south US-31 2.6 miles to the traffic light at Lake, (the next light after passing a softball field, on the right).

Turn west onto Lake and go one block to Bay Front Drive, on the right, just before city hall and the river. Turn right (north) onto Bay Front and then immediately turn right (east) again onto Depot Court, which leads into a parking area behind the Little Traverse History Museum.

1

From the parking area, head back to Lake Street and cross over to a cream-and-rust-colored Victorian-looking pavilion, a remnant of a turn-of-the-century health spa complex, where tourists soaked in sulfurous mineral waters reputed to cure kidney trouble, indigestion and other ailments. A nearby drinking fountain still continuously dispenses an ice-cold flow of mineral water.

The fast-flowing, 20-foot-wide river here divides around a small, grassy island then drops five feet over Mitchell Dam, a specially designed spillway that keeps lampreys from invading upstream. The dam also stops fish from running the river, and so in spring and fall the area is crowded with anglers tossing lures at trout and salmon. From the dam the river whitewaters through a 75-yard-long chute to the bay.

From the pavilion, head south on the sidewalk along the east bank past some large, old maples to the historic bridge (p. 108) that carries Mitchell Street (US-31) over the river. Cross under the bridge to a wide dirt path that is edged in spots, in season, with the tiny, blue petals of Forget-Me-Nots.

Fifteen yards beyond the bridge, the trail passes the first of many large, mature Sugar Maples, this one leaning precariously over the river. Ten yards farther is an even bigger specimen, on the right, followed in just a few steps by a clump of formidable, healthy to moribund White Birch, on the left, plus a dozen or so impressive Black Walnuts spaced over the next 50 yards.

At 0.1 miles the route crosses a dirt drainage trough imbedded with large concrete chunks to minimize erosion during heavy storm-water runoff from the streets above. From here the wide dirt path continues to follow the river closely, about 10 feet above, as it passes beneath a canopy formed by maples, walnuts, ash, and a few Box Elders.

At 0.2 miles — just a few feet past a trail that branches off toward the river and just before breaking out into a semiopen area — a lone Horse Chestnut has sprouted at the trail's edge, on the right. Though only an inch in diameter and 12 feet tall, the sapling's characteristic tear-drop-shaped, palm-looking leaves already measure 6-8 inches long and 2-3 inches across.

The trail from here bears away from the river, and as it rises gently but steadily over the next quarter mile, you lose sight, but rarely the sound of the rushing water. Several side trails in that stretch head toward the water.

A few yards past the chestnut, the path crosses a semiopen grassy meadow and, at ¼ mile, encounters a large deadfall. The huge limb, split off from a large maple, forms an arch high enough that minimal ducking is required to pass beneath.

From the deadfall the path enters the shade of a grove of mature maples then, at 0.4 miles, reaches a section where grapevine-laced undergrowth crowds the trail and the forest type changes to predominantly willow and aspen. It's here that the river comes back into view from 25-30 feet above it, across from a stairway down the steep west bank. And it's here — where the songs of birds compete with and sometimes win out over the roar of the river — that it's easiest to forget you're in the middle of a city bustling with tourists and traffic.

As the trail approaches a power line, shoulder-high sumac — whose characteristic large, erect clusters of red late-summer fruit were used by American Indians to make a lemonade-type drink — predominates the undergrowth.

The trail crosses under the power line, passes a huge willow on the left, breaks out onto an open, grassy bank, then forks. Bear right (the trail to the left leads up to city streets) and descend to a pedestrian bridge. A vantage point about halfway across the 100-yard stretch looks down 20 feet at a small but dramatic waterfall created as the rushing, roiling river drops three feet over a rock ledge, then immediately drops another foot before rushing away in a whitewater rapids.

Unobstructed looks at long upstream and downstream stretches of the clear, shallow, tea-colored river come from the center of the pedestrian bridge.

Across the bridge the route reaches the junction of several trails and trailroads. The routes left follow the river 0.6 miles to the Sheridan Road Bridge; the trails to the right head back a half mile along the river to the dam.

The path that hugs the shore to the left is a 125-yard bushwhack, with tricky footing until joining a trailroad above. The wide gravel path that heads right (north) and up from the bridge connects directly with the trailroad in 50 yards, at a pair of stately spruce. From there, double back left (south), following the wide gravel road.

Fifteen yards down the road, up to the right is a false-fronted historic building undergoing renovation by the Little Traverse Historical Society. Built in the mid-1880s, the single-story structure originally housed a meat market and later, around 1910, was used by the fire department as a place to dry, maintain and store their canvas hoses.

A hundred ten yards farther, in the open on both sides of the road, are small stands of young Lombardy Poplar, recognized by their unique slim, upswept profiles.

A hundred yards farther, the road skirts a baseball field, on the right. Just past home plate, bear left as far as possible, passing beneath and by two imposing Box Elders onto a mowed grassy area, then follow close to the bank's edge for peeks at the river.

A few yards farther, more-open views of the river come from the Bridge Street bridge area, especially in spring and fall when the prevalent shoulder- to head-high sumac is leafless. At all times, echoing underneath the bridge amplifies and intensifies the sounds of the rushing river.

About 200 yards past the bridge, the route curves through an open area where

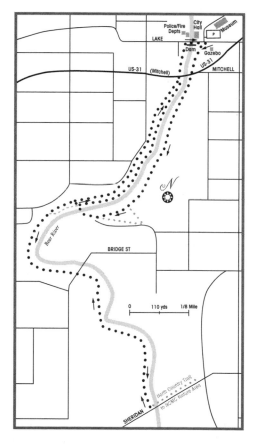

rocks, sand, gravel, picnic tables, metal bleachers, wood chips, dead limbs, and other materials are temporarily stored by the city's Department of Public Works.

The route follows the road along a power line here then — where the river makes a 90-degree bend left — veers left to the riverbank on an obvious, wide, wood-chip-covered trail that plunges into the shade of thick willow, ash, and Box Elder, including several good-size representatives of the latter that lean over the path. In summer the thick growth and under-growth nearly blocks the sights and sounds of light- to medium-industry complexes that line the banks across the river.

Seventy-five yards in, among the several kinds of willow that grow here are several dozen specimens of a unique, unidentified variety whose inch-long fruit resembles green pine cones when new, and tiny, gray beehives when old and dry. The unusual 10-foot-tall shrubs edge the route until it again becomes canopied by a stand of Box Elder.

A hundred seventy-five yards farther, the trail breaks out onto grassy banks that line the Sheridan Road bridge, which is punctuated at its west end by an enor-mous, distinctly barked willow.

To return to Mineral Well Park, first backtrack to the junction of the trails and trailroads near the large spruces above the pedestrian bridge. From there you can drop to the water-hugging shore trail or take the easier-walking high road, both running approximately 0.4 miles along the river's west bank.

The wide, gravel service road heads east along a split-rail fence 75 yards to an over-look, with picturesque views of the bridge, river and waterfall. (Thirty stairs drop from the overlook 20 feet to the shore

trail.) From here the near-level road gradu-ally winds north, following the river, with glimpses of it through mostly maples.

A hundred twenty-five yards from the overlook, the road drops steeply but briefly to an open, grassy area. From there, con-tinue following the gravel road ¼ mile back to Mitchell Dam and Mineral Well Park or bear sharply right 15-20 yards to connect with the shore trail (see paragraph after next).

From the pedestrian bridge, the west-bank shore trail drops across the open, grassy hillside to the foot of the overlook stairs. For the next 75 yards, the trail near-ly touches the river and turns rocky as it passes through an area of thick under-brush, where walking can be tough, tricky and sometimes damp. Closing in on the trail are a variety of (flowering, in season) bushes and shrubs, backed by maple, ash, willow, birch and basswood.

The trail breaks out of the dense growth onto a narrow, 50-yard-long strip of mead-ow that edges the river then briefly rises be-tween towering willows to a grassy plateau (and the junction with the trailroad route). Bear sharply right, to the east edge of the field, then turn left (north) and cross the 75-yard-long stretch, staying as close as possible to the river. Over the last 10 yards the path passes a mixture of basswood, sugar maple, white pine, and ash, on the right, then drops to a second, even-larger grassy field.

Continue straight (north), again staying as close to the river as possible, 150 yards to the far end of the grassy area, marked by five recently planted mountain ash. From there veer left, rise to the gravel service road, and follow it 75 yards to where it veers left, directly in front of a behemoth 2-foot-diameter, near-100-foot-tall spruce

that stands guard in front of the bridge. Bear to the right of the silent sentinel and walk the river's edge next to a 50-yard-long sidewalk-looking concrete hump, a remnant from one of the long-ago commercial activities here.

The route then passes under the center of the bridge between two sets of the massive concrete supporting columns and follows the river flow back to the dam.

Bear River Nature Trail

An easy-walking trail that passes through widely diverse habitats and forest communities as it traverses the east side of the Bear River Valley then drops to close encounters with the river.

ROUND TRIP 2.4 MILES
ALLOW 1½ HOURS

Facilities: Restrooms are located in college buildings. Rest benches are spaced along the trail.

Directions: From the junction of US-31 and US-131, go south on US-131 0.5 miles to Sheridan. Turn left onto Sheridan and go ¾ miles to a dead end at Howard Street. Turn right (south) onto Howard and go 0.2 miles to the entrance to North Central Michigan College, marked by a large blue sign. Turn left (east) onto the entrance road and wind 0.3 miles to a T intersection. Turn right (south), go ½ block, and turn into a parking lot, on the left (east). Park here and, on foot, drop over the grassy knoll on the south side of the parking lot and follow a wide, woodchip-covered, rock-lined path that runs behind (east of) the Institute for Business and Industry Training building about 175 yards south to the trailhead.

Facing the trailhead sign, take the rock-lined, leftmost path, heading east. The trail immediately crosses a tiny brook, cuts through a small open area spiked with short cedars, and winds on a boardwalk past a few young Scotch Pine (likely the wind-borne offspring of a couple along the Russian Creek Trail, p. 9). The path then cuts through a small cedar thicket to — at 200 yards from the trailhead — a clearing being reclaimed by nature. Fifteen-foot-tall cedars, 5- to 10-foot-tall Pin and Black Cherry saplings, Bracken Ferns and other "pioneer" species have sprouted in the open, sunny area. Here they will help stabilize the soil and provide food and cover for animals before being replaced by longer-living, shade-tolerant species.

Especially interesting are the Black Cherry trees, identifiable by their rough, flaky, dark bark, often described as looking like burnt potato chips. Supposedly, a natural wild-cherry-syrup cough medicine can be extracted from the bark, but the foliage and twigs contain hydrocyanic acid, which is poisonous to humans and animals. Much larger specimens intermittently edge the rest of the route, with several congregated near the junction with the North Country Trail at ¾ mile.

A few wood-reinforced dirt steps drop through the cedar/cherry opening, and 75 yards farther a rest bench marks the junction with the NCMC to Lockwood Park trail (p. 15). A wide, wildflower-filled meadow spills from the bench 75 yards down to a wetland. Follow the well-worn, sandy path straight ahead as it gently rises, falls, and wiggles through another open area that in summer is canopied by a thick growth of waist-high Bracken Ferns.

At ¼ mile the path drops then rises through the cool shade of a cedar thicket to a 150-yard-long bouncing boardwalk that traces the edge of a 52-acre Northern White Cedar swamp, on the right. The cold, dark mixture of wood and muck appears to be near impenetrable and inhospitable. But the swamp provides winter shelter and food for deer and other wildlife. And the springs that moisten the ground nearly year round continually help replenish the river.

Just a few yards past the end of the boardwalk and just before a bench on the left, a well-trod path through the grass to the right leads 15 feet to a small oval of stones that create a tiny pool around one of the swamp area's many bubbling springs. White sand roils from several small inlets in the bottom, and a small stream falls off quickly from the pool into the swamp to ultimately join the Bear River. On sunny summer days, surface-skimming insects named Water Striders cast shadows onto the mostly moss-covered bottom.

Across the trail at 0.4 miles, a rest bench marks the beginning of a grove of White Pine — some reaching 60-70 feet in height, and 18-20 inches in diameter — that were planted on the ridge, possibly by the farmer who owned the land 100 years ago, to prevent erosion.

As the trail leaves the pine plantation, the boughs of young, 6- to 10-foot-tall Tamaracks poke into and over the trail, gradually increasing in number over the

next few yards to a small stand of a dozen and a half, on the right, just before another rest bench. The evergreen-looking tree is easily recognized by its soft, feathery needles, which turn yellow and drop in the fall. American Indians used the trees' slender roots to stitch together strips of birch bark for their canoes.

Touching the trail's edge 20 yards before another bench on the left is a good-size granite boulder, most likely carried from Canada and left here by glaciers some 12,000 years ago. Several smaller companions are scattered up the needle-covered slope, and a few others are potential toe-stubbers embedded in the trail itself.

The bench fronts a thicket of Largetooth (Bigtooth) Aspen, a smooth-barked, fast-growing tree that colonizes open areas created by fire, farming, logging or other disturbances. Because of the symmetrical, rounded profile of this group and the ability of the species to readily sprout up new

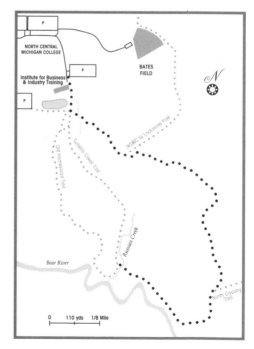

trees from its root system, it's likely all these ash are clones, that is genetically identical.

Across the trail, a large, open meadow is filled with grass-looking sedges and wildflowers, including the potentially sneeze-producing goldenrod and the large, white, flat-topped Queen Anne's Lace (also called Wild Carrot).

The narrow, well-worn path skirts the east side of the meadow, then gently rises and falls while winding past the cedar swamp, on the right, under the cool shade (even at noon in summer) provided by a mixture of trees on the left. Blotting out the sun are Tamarack, pine, birch, cedar, and a few huge Sugar Maples, but with Largetooth Aspen predominating, some reaching enormous size of up to 18 inches in diameter and 50 feet in height.

Just past a rest bench at ¾ mile, the route reaches a junction with a section of the North Country Trail, which when completed will run continuously from the Appalachian Trail in Maine 3,200 miles to the Lewis and Clark Trail in North Dakota. (The section that branches off left here rises to and across a farm field to connect with Greenwood Road.) Continue straight, following the combined North Country/Bear River trail another 175 yards to where it cuts across a clearing beneath a power line.

A few yards farther, the trail cuts across a meadow surrounded by pine and filled in season with blooming goldenrod, white Daisy Fleabane, yellow Common Buttercup, and purple Spotted Knapweed.

The trail then loops back around under the power line, where it meets the Bear River about 12 feet above it. Beginning more than 11 miles upstream as the outflow of Walloon (formerly Bear) Lake, the river to here has taken in Haymarsh and Spring Brook creeks and drained an estimated 10,000-12,000 acres of forest, farmland and wetlands. Tea-colored from tannins leached from the swamps, the shallow, 20- to 25-foot-wide stream here moves slowly but strongly around large, gentle bends, as though taking a deep breath before beginning its final dramatic plunge to the bay ½ mile later.

From the river overlook the trail passes through a small Largetooth and Trembling (Quaking) Aspen thicket, then cedar, as it drops to a throwback walkway constructed of round cedar logs, not the ubiquitous, contemporary pressure-treated planks. The short logwalk crosses one of the area's many brooks, and for the next 100 yards the trail traces the riverbank, with open views of the flow from many spots.

The route then turns away into the shade of Balsam Fir, Eastern Hemlock, Sugar Maple, aspen, Northern White Cedar, and a few virgin Eastern White Pine, including a couple of imposing, century-plus-old specimens that escaped lumbermen's axes.

Just past the pines, the trail drops into the dark fringes of the cedar swamp and, at 1.2 miles, reaches a picturesque bridge across Russian Creek. The clear waters of the shallow, 3-foot-wide creek flow over a white-sand bottom and twist around, through, and over a tangle of roots and small deadfalls to join the river 50 yards away.

The bridge also marks the junction with North Central Michigan College's Old Homestead (p. 12) and Russian Creek (p. 9) nature trails, and it's possible to return to the trailhead using one of those routes. However, by retracing your steps on the Bear River Trail, you'll likely see different things and see things differently.

RUSSIAN CREEK TRAIL

Carry field guides while walking this short, perpetually damp, sometimes-wet bottomland trail to the Bear River. More than 100 species of vegetation help form this mostly natural arboretum, including nearly four dozen different kinds of trees, shrubs and wildflowers in just the first 200 yards.

The area is also rife with deer and well-worn deer walkways.

ROUND TRIP 1.0 MILE

ALLOW 30 MINUTES WITHOUT FIELD GUIDES, 2-3 HOURS WITH

Facilities: Restrooms are available in campus buildings. Rest benches are spaced along the trail.

Directions: From the junction of US-31 and US-131, go south on US-131 0.5 miles to Sheridan. Turn left onto Sheridan and go ¾ miles to a deadend at Howard Street. Turn right (south) onto Howard and go 0.2 miles to the entrance to North Central Michigan College, marked by a large blue sign. Turn left (east) onto the entrance road and wind 0.3 miles to a T intersection. Turn right (south), go ½ block, and turn into a parking lot, on the left (east). Park here and, on foot, drop over the grassy knoll on the south side of the parking lot and follow a wide, woodchip-covered, rock-lined path that runs behind (east of) the Institute for Business and Industry Training building about 175 yards south to the trailhead.

Start at the manmade marsh about 20 yards in front (northwest) of the trailhead sign. Created by North Central Michigan College personnel just a dozen years ago, the 200- by 40-foot oblong, shallow pond has already evolved into a classic example of how all lakes and other contained water bodies fill in to ultimately become terra firma.

The process is efficient. The water body fills with runoff sediment and with vegetation that grows, dies, falls to the bottom and produces peat until the depression is so full that surface water no longer stands in it. The time it takes depends on the size and depth of the water body and whether there are feeder streams or underground springs.

And the process is orderly. Cattails, rushes, and other aquatic plants grow first, fronted quickly by Water Lilies, Duckweed, and other floating plants. When the peat their decayed remains creates becomes solid enough around the edges, water-loving shrubs, then trees such as Tamarack and willow take over, which forces the aquatic plants farther out into the water.

These concentric rings of vegetation types also tend to make the remains of the original water body round, no matter its original shape. When outer rings have encroached to the point that there's no longer

characteristically divided at the base into many thick, crooked branches. The path drops briefly, then levels out as it passes between a couple of small Northern White Cedars, by thick growth of Speckled Alder (named because of the many horizontal, off-white or light-orange markings on its thin, reddish-brown bark), and through a small grove of Scotch Pine formed by a couple of mature trees plus several smaller offspring. On the left just before the trail moves through a pair of pines into a brief opening is a Pin Cherry, also known as Fire Cherry because its seedlings are often the first to sprout after a forest fire.

Twenty yards across the clearing the trail forks. Take the left fork (straight) through an alder thicket and out into a semiopen area filled, in season, with blooming goldenrod and Queen Anne's Lace. Towering over the 25-yard-long meadow at its edges are a few old white pines.

For the next 20 yards the route is intermittently canopied by alders, a few Pin Cherries and, from each side just before breaking out into a clearing, two Glossy Buckthorns that arch over the trail, especially in late summer when heavy with dark-blue berries. A few yards farther, on the left fronting a stand of white pine, is a grove of ash, likely Red Ash, which prefer this type of lowland habitat. The species, with its characteristic alternate, compound leaves,(see illustration, following page) predominates over the next 150 yards and is well represented throughout the rest of the area.

The trail then gently winds for 20 yards through a semiopen area, where a dozen scattered, stunted apple trees are surrounded by goldenrod and Queen Anne's lace plus an occasional milkweed, white Daisy Fleabane, and purple Spotted Knapweed.

enough water to support the aquatic plants, the water body has officially become a swamp, which eventually will become dry land.

The pond here is in the middle stages of filling in. Willows are spaced around the shore, cattails are encroaching from the edges, and the open water is covered with Duckweed and, often, ducks. (An occasional muskrat and turtle have also been spotted swimming here.)

The largest growth of cattails is on the west and east (elongated) ends as they gradually reshape the open water to a circle. Near the southwest corner, a well-worn corridor cuts through the cattails, and when you walk on it you experience the unique, slightly uneasy feeling of the not-yet-completely-solid soil shifting underfoot.

From the pond, return (south) and take the trail to the immediate right (west) of the trailhead sign, which is backed by a lone Box Elder that, though small, has

Ten feet off the trail on the right, just before the path plunges again into a thicket is a 30-foot-tall Tamarack, a tree that, though evergreen looking, drops its needles in fall.

The route then passes between a couple of clumps of white birch and, at 0.2 miles, enters a short, needle-carpeted section created by a pair of large white pines. A few steps farther, about 20 feet off the trail on the right, is an enormous multitrunked basswood.

From there the trail briefly drops, then levels out about 10 feet above a wetland, on the left, and is lined on the right with young basswoods, identifiable by their large, round leaves. At 0.3 miles, the path divides and gradually drops as it cuts through a 100-yard-long, open strip blanketed with waist- to shoulder-high ferns. Take the higher, drier rightmost path.

At the trail's edge on the right, where the trails rejoin is a 6-inch-diameter Hop-Hornbeam, whose bark looks like it was put through a paper shredder then stuck in strips to the trunk. Not far into the woods on the right, as you face this tree — named because its fruit clusters resemble the beer ingredient, hops — are other, smaller specimens.

The trail — now lined on the left by cedar and on the right by a variety of shrubs and trees — gradually descends another 100 yards to meet Russian Creek,

which sweeps out of the swamp from the left. From here to its end 175 yards later, the path closely follows the creek, passing on the left at 70 yards a trio of 30-foot-tall, moribund Black Cherry trees, recognized by their dark, flakey "burnt potato chip" bark. Thirty yards farther, the path plunges into the cool, dark depths of the cedar swamp and curves 75 yards to a footbridge across the picturesque, quick-flowing creek, complete with miniwaterfalls formed by fallen limbs.

The bridge also marks the junction with North Central Michigan College's Old Homestead (p. 12) and Bear River (p. 6) nature trails, and it's possible to return to the trailhead using one of those routes. But because this trail is short and re-examination can be rewarding, backtrack to the trailhead and take the other routes separately.

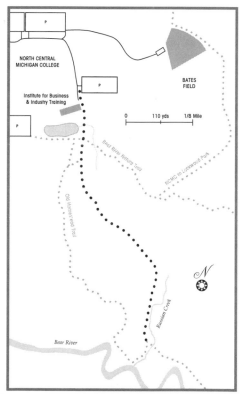

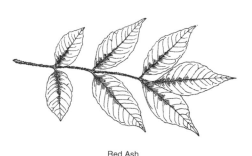

Red Ash

OLD HOMESTEAD TRAIL

Distinct specimens of ash, Hop-Hornbeam, White Birch and Sugar Maple are highlights along this trail, which leads to close-up views of the Bear River and a small creek that feeds it. The route also explores a portion of 120 acres purchased here in 1877 by Russian immigrant Abraham Seibert who, with his family, farmed and worked the land for the next 41 years.

ROUND TRIP 1.2 MILES

ALLOW 1 HOUR

Facilities: Restrooms are available in campus buildings. Rest benches are spaced along the trail.

Directions: From the junction of US-31 and US-131, go south on US-131 0.5 miles to Sheridan. Turn left onto Sheridan and go ¾ miles to a deadend at Howard Street. Turn right (south) onto Howard and go 0.2 miles to the entrance to North Central Michigan College, marked by a large blue sign. Turn left (east) onto the entrance road and wind 0.3 miles to a T intersection. Turn right (south), go ½ block, and turn into a parking lot, on the left (east). Park here and, on foot, drop over the grassy knoll on the south side of the parking lot and follow a wide, woodchip-covered, rock-lined path that runs behind (east of) the Institute for Business and Industry Training building about 175 yards south to the trailhead.

Take the path that drops to the immediate right (west) of the trailhead sign and go straight (south), 50 yards to a fork. Take the right (westmost) path, which marks the interface between a large, grassy, wild-flower-filled meadow on the right and, on the left, a dense thicket of Speckled Alder, so named because of the many horizontal, off-white or light-orange markings on its thin, reddish-brown bark. The shrubs' tangle of contorted stems and its wetland habitat make for an ideal sanctuary for Woodcock, Common Yellowthroat, and other birds and wildlife. Fifty yards farther, young pines crowd the trail, partially shielding the alder thicket from view.

A few yards farther, on the left at the end of a short boardwalk that cuts through the thicket, is a pile of rocks, probably originally scattered over the area by melting glaciers some 12,000 years ago, then cleared and placed here by the farm owners more than a century ago.

The trail rises steeply for the next 30 yards, then breaks into the open atop a wide ridge that drops precipitously to the Bear River, on the right, and gradually to a swamp, on the left. Just a few yards farther, past a clump of low-growing junipers and a rest bench on the left, the path drops steeply but briefly to an impressive ash, on the left at ¼ mile. Each of the double trunks of this specimen — most likely a white ash, which prefers this upland habitat — measures almost 2 feet in diameter.

Seventy-five yards farther, a rest bench on the left fronts a grassy meadow that sweeps up to the forested ridge. Though this opening was cleared and used for four decades as the Seiberts' homesite, no signs of their presence remain.

The trail gently drops over the next 125 yards to a rapid succession of remarkable trees beginning with a huge White Birch clump, on the left, formed by five trunks, conjoined at their base and each measuring 40-50 feet tall and 12 to 14 inches in diameter. A hundred feet farther is a uniquely burled Sugar Maple, about five feet off the trail on the right. If this tree stood in harvestable forest, the half dozen large, distinctive swirled-grained knots about 10 feet up the trunk might be turned into bowls, artwork or veneer.

On opposite sides of the path 50 feet farther is a pair of Hop-Hornbeams, layered with characteristic bark that looks like it has been put through a paper shredder then glued to the trunk. The iron-strong

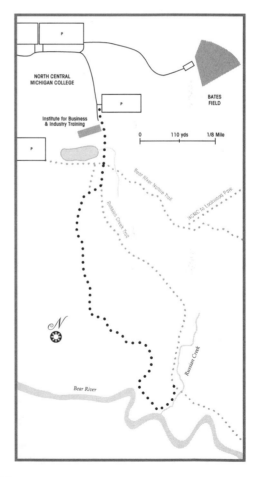

wood of these trees' forebears may well have been used by the Seiberts to fashion tool handles, fence posts, and even wagon wheels and sleigh runners. They're followed by a much larger specimen, on the right, just before a bench set up to view a hydra-shaped, 70-foot-tall, 4-foot-diameter behemoth Sugar Maple whose scores of limbs snake up from head height.

The trail then cuts through a stand of Trembling (Quaking) Aspen as it drops to a 20-yard-long boardwalk that winds through a thick, dark cedar swamp.

At ½ mile the trail breaks out from the boardwalk to an open overlook 10 feet above an oxbow bend in the Bear River. Beginning more than 11 miles upstream as the outflow of Walloon (formerly Bear) Lake, the river to here has taken in Haymarsh and Spring Brook creeks and drained an estimated 10,000-12,000 acres of forest, farmland and swamp. In summer

here, the shallow, slow-moving flow is often covered by darting Water Striders, insects whose long, hair-thin, hair-covered legs allow them to literally walk on water.

The main trail bears left, briefly away from the flow, to another short boardwalk, followed by a brief section of dirt path, then another short boardwalk that leads up to a fork. The path branching right leads to a rest bench that provides another perspective of the meandering, tea-colored river. The main trail continues another 10 yards to where Russian Creek empties into the river. The small but quick-flowing creek has formed a minidelta here by continuously depositing white sand it has carried from above. However, the creek outlet is on the outside of a bend in the Bear, where the 25-foot-wide river's strong force carries away most of the sand, making the delta's further growth a literal wash.

From there, the trail turns left onto a boardwalk that follows the creek's clear waters and white-sand bottom into the otherwordly looking cedar swamp it helps drain. The walkway winds 50 yards past several miniwaterfalls created by fallen limbs to a footbridge and the junction with North Central Michigan College's Bear River (p. 6) and Russian Creek (p. 9) nature trails. It's possible to return to the trailhead using one of those routes, but to see different things and see things differently along the Old Homestead Trail, walk it back to the trailhead.

NCMC
TO LOCKWOOD PARK

A diverse route that loops through the fringes of a quiet, scenic nature preserve then rises — with sweeping views of the Bear River Valley — to a "peak" look at Little Traverse Bay.

ROUND TRIP 2¼ MILES (2 miles via the Bates Field return)

ALLOW 1½ HOURS

Facilities: Restrooms are located in college buildings. Concessions and restrooms at Bates Park are open during game times. A convenience store/deli is located at the northeast corner of Kalamazoo and Jennings.

Directions: From the junction of US-31 and US-131, go south on US-131 0.5 miles to Sheridan. Turn left onto Sheridan and go ¾ miles to a deadend at Howard Street. Turn right (south) onto Howard and go 0.2 miles to the entrance to North Central Michigan College, marked by a large blue sign. Turn left (east) onto the entrance road and wind 0.3 miles to a T intersection. Turn right (south), go ½ block, and turn into a parking lot, on the left (east). Park here and, on foot, drop over the grassy knoll on the south side of the parking lot and follow a wide, woodchip-covered, rock-lined path that runs behind (east of) the Institute for Business and Industry Training building about 175 yards south to the trailhead.

The first 275 yards of this route follows NCMC's Bear River Nature Trail (p. 6).

Facing the trailhead sign, take the left-most path east 200 yards to a few wood-reinforced dirt steps down. Seventy-five yards farther (10 yards before reaching a rest bench, on the left), veer left (northeast) along the east edge of a stand of cedar on a faint path through a small, grassy, fern-filled field. From the north edge of the field the trail becomes more obvious as it rises steeply then moderately northeast through predominantly cedar mixed with a few birch, Sugar Maple, and the uniquely strip-barked Hop-hornbeam.

At 0.2 miles the still-rising trail cuts through a more-open area filled with waist- to shoulder-high ferns then, 50 yards farther, veers left (north) and levels off as it briefly skirts a large farm field, on the right (east). In that stretch, the trail passes three enormous Largetooth Aspens followed quickly by a pair of even-larger smooth-barked beech.

There, the trail veers away from the working field and drops steeply under a canopy of maples and beech to the bottom of a deep, long ravine created by retreating glaciers some 12,000 years ago. A battle-ship-size piece of ice likely broke off from the main glacial sheet, which while melting then washed tons of earthen glacial debris around and possibly even over the mam-moth chunk. When the orphaned, insulated ice block itself later melted, it left this ¼-mile-long, 75-foot wide molded depression.

The rock-strewn trail crosses the ravine at its deepest point, about 30 feet, but on a sidewalk-wide, 10-foot-high earthen, apparently manmade bridge.

At ⅓ mile, at the top on the opposite side, the route reaches a fork. The wide path to the left is the first of several well-worn to faint side trails that lead generally northwest toward three new (1999) youth baseball fields, which come into occasional view over the next quarter mile.

The main trail continues straight (north), dipping and rising briefly then breaking out through a small thicket of Largetooth Aspen onto a grassy plateau. The trail continues straight (north) about 125 yards across the open area — spiked with young pines, cedars, and other trees and shrubs — to a trail intersection. (The rightmost path rises sharply east just a few yards to a private subdivision. The path straight ahead dead-ends in a thicket.)

Bear left (northwest), rising 20 yards to another fork, marked by a post, at 0.45 miles. Continue straight (northwest) onto a wide, grassy two-track that passes through a Scotch Pine plantation 175 yards to a wide, open, grassy knoll. (On the return route, two options are available from this point, marked "O" on the map.) Bear right (north) 50 yards across the knoll toward a large, green utility box and the junction with a wide dirt road, closed to vehicle traffic.

Turn sharply right (east) onto the road, which drops briefly between large rocks, crosses over a wetland, passes an elevated storm-sewer manhole, then rises moderately to large rocks that block vehicle access from the corner of Atkins and Kalamazoo, at 0.7 miles. Looking back about halfway up, views sweep from south to north across the Bear River Valley, over the NCMC campus to the high southwest outskirts of Petoskey, and up the face of a high bluff that helps define the southern limit of city residences.

Turn left (north) onto Kalamazoo, which rises moderately and steadily nearly ¼ mile to an intersection with Jennings. Lining the west side of the street and providing morning shade to residents there are more than a dozen huge, old Norway Spruces.

At Jennings turn left (west) and go one block to Seldon. Turn right (north) onto Seldon and go one block to Spruce. Cross Spruce, take the asphalt then concrete sidewalk into Lockwood Park, and head up either stairs or grass to the obvious hilly high point, about 20 yards north. From here — one of the city's highest spots, some 250 feet above the bay — views (p. *x*) are good any time but are exceptional during fall color. And during leafless seasons, horizons are literally broadened.

From the peak, backtrack 0.6 miles to junction "O," on the grassy knoll. From there either retrace the half mile-plus route back to the ravine and through the nature

preserve or take the following shorter quarter-mile route.

At "O," bear right (southwest) and go 75 yards through a wide swath between pines (the baseball complex, Bates Field, is in view straight ahead), then drop another 75 yards, between a pine grove on the right and an outfield on the left, to the recreational complex's hub.

There, bear right, go southwest through a small handicapped-only parking area, then follow the asphalt road west to the park's entrance pillars. Just a few feet farther, bear left onto a sidewalk that winds a few yards to the parking lot behind the Institute for Business and Industry Training building.

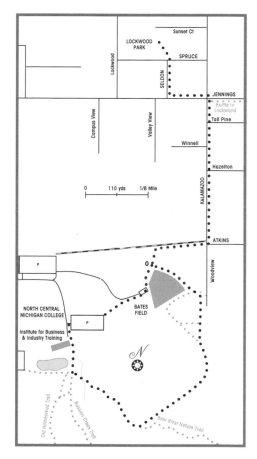

THE KETTLE TO LOCKWOOD PARK

An open walk inside a transient, prehistoric lake followed by a steady 75-foot rise to views of the bay from one of the city's high points.

ROUND TRIP 2.8 MILES

ALLOW 1½ HOURS

Facilities: A convenience store/deli is located at the northeast corner of Kalamazoo and Jennings.

Directions: From the junction of US-31 and US-131, drive north then east on north US-31 0.7 miles to a traffic signal at Mitchell Street (the first signal after crossing the Mitchell Street Bridge and curving left, north). Turn right (east) onto Mitchell and go 1.1 miles to the entrance to Petoskey High School, at Hill Road.

Or from the junction of US-31 and M-119 go west on south US-31 0.7 miles to Division Road, 0.4 miles past the traffic light at Glens Shopping Plaza. Turn left (south) onto Division and go 0.8 miles to Mitchell Road. Turn right (west) onto Mitchell Road and go 0.5 miles to the entrance to Petoskey High School, at Hill Road.

Turn south onto Hill and go two blocks to a fork. Bear right, curving east on Hill just a few yards to a parking lot on the right (north), east of the tennis courts.

From the west end of the parking lot, drop west on Hill about 125 yards to a small wetland on the right (north), just past the west end of the tennis courts. The 2-acre vegetation-filled area is all that remains of a lake created some 12,000 years ago during the recession of the last of the great continental glaciers that covered this area. As the mile-thick glacier retreated, a much-thinner block of ice may have broken off from the edge of the main sheet here. Water from the higher, melting parent glacier then washed millions of tons of till — earthen debris gouged, scraped up and carried by the ice from Canada — around the sides and possibly even over the top of the separated chunk. When the insulated ice orphan itself later melted, it left a huge depression called a "kettle hole."

Kettle hole sides, however, are usually steeper then those here, so it is possible instead that several of the melting glacier's snouts dumped their load of boulders, pebbles, sand and clay in an oval of adjacent 75-foot high mounds, called moraines.

Whichever way glaciers formed this basin, it then temporarily — in geologic time — filled with meltwater that covered this area to levels hundreds of feet higher than current Great Lakes levels. In the ensuing centuries the earth here rebounded, that is rose back up, after being depressed by the glaciers' tremendous weight. During that time, the pre-Great Lakes' water levels dropped, and an outlet that ran from the lake to the bay wore deeper. As a result, the lake here drained north to the bay until it emptied, leaving only the spring- and drainage-fed wetland and an unusual small creek that runs from it (see p. 24 for more details).

From the wetland the route follows a sidewalk on the south side of Hill that rises 175 yards east to a driveway in front of the high school. The route follows a sidewalk along the curved driveway east to the school's building trades program area, where students construct homes that are then sold and moved.

There the sidewalk turns right (south) along Northmen Drive and rises gently then moderately 200 yards to a small fitness court, on the right. There, graphics and instructions show and explain eight different body-conditioning, cardiovascular-fitness, weight-control, strength-training, and aerobic exercises. Picturesquely set behind (east of) a thick pine grove up and back across the road to the left (east) is the United Methodist Church.

At a half mile the route passes the Middle School, on the left, then gently drops 225 yards to a concrete rest bench — accompanied only by a large, lone boulder — set in an open, grassy field to the right. The wide area sweeps from the overlook down to what was the deepest part of the prehistoric lake.

Over the next 250 yards the walkway rises and drops, then rises moderately but steadily for the remaining 0.6 miles of the route, which gradually curves west past the grassy, wildflower-filled area, on the right. On the left (south), working farm fields sweep up to a large, red barn and pair of

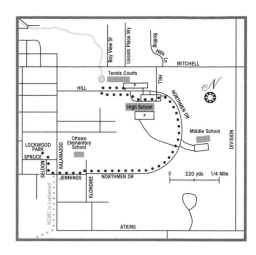

silos that sit on what for a time would have been the prehistoric lake's south shore.

The asphalt path then passes a small clump of woods on the right, followed by an old barn, also on the right about a half block before Northmen Drive ends at a junction with Klondike. The route jogs (left) along Klondike just a few feet then turns right (west) and follows Jennings 0.2 miles across Kalamazoo to Seldon. Turn right (north) onto Seldon and go one block to Spruce. Cross Spruce, take the asphalt then concrete sidewalk into Lockwood Park, and head up either stairs or grass to the turnaround spot, an obvious hilly high point, about 20 yards north.

From here — one of the city's highest spots, nearly 250 feet above the bay — views (p. x) are good any time but are exceptional during fall color. And during leafless seasons, horizons are literally broadened.

BAY FRONT PARK TO BAY VIEW

A near-level, open walk at the bay's edge, with near-continuous, continually changing views over the water (p. x). The route also passes a picturesque waterfall and a row of imposing Victorian "cottages" that front one of Michigan's most unique and historic summer communities.

Beginning 125 years ago, the waterfront along this walk was a near-mile-long strip of industry and commerce. A quarry operation blasted out pieces of the bluff, and several on-site kilns processed the chunks into limestone. Ships carried away not only the limestone but also lumber, Great Lakes fish and, briefly, hundreds of thousands of passenger pigeons, which were served as a delicacy at restaurants.

The pigeons were slaughtered to extinction, kilns closed, and lumber, fish, and other raw resources were depleted. But tourism thrived, and as a result, the shore area here was gradually reclaimed and developed into a linear public park.

ROUND TRIP 2.9 MILES

ALLOW 2 HOURS

Facilities: Restrooms and water are available at the park building next to (just west of) the softball field. A concession area there is open during event times only. Oleson's is a full-service grocery store with restrooms for use by their customers.

Directions:From the junction of US-31 and US-131, drive north then east on north US-31 0.7 miles to a traffic signal at Lake Street (the second signal after crossing the Mitchell Street Bridge and curving left, north). Or from the junction of M-119 and US-31, drive west on south US-31 2.6 miles to the traffic light at Lake, (the next light after passing a softball field, on the right).

Turn west onto Lake and go one block to Bay Front Drive, on the right, just before city hall and the river. Turn right (north) onto Bay Front and then immediately turn right (east) again onto Depot Court, which leads into a parking area behind the Little Traverse Historical Museum.

From the east edge of the museum parking lot, head east on an asphalt path that winds along the base of a 20-foot-high bluff 125 yards to Bayfront Drive. Until a century ago, the Bear River emptied into the bay here. But in 1894 the rivermouth was relocated some 150 yards west, and the Chicago and Western Railroad then filled in the old channel and a portion of the bay to create the site for their Victorian-style passenger depot, which now houses the museum (p. 107).

At Bayfront Drive the path edges the road for 30 yards east to Bayfront Park's main promenade — a wide, flag- and bench-lined, cobbled-brick and concrete walkway that stretches north to a clock tower and marina pier. A tunnel to the right (south), here, connects to the Gaslight Shopping District (p. 104).

Continue east another 50 yards then

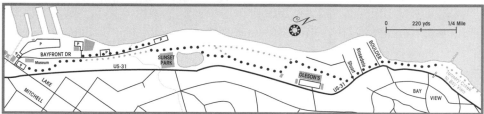

cross over to the north side of Bayfront Drive at a one-diamond fast-pitch softball complex, which occupies the sight of a former kiln. In summer, games are played most weekday nights and throughout the day and evenings on Saturdays and Sundays. Home runs hit over the left field fence plop into the bay.

Continue straight (east) along the sidewalk, which parallels the bay 30-40 yards from it. (The asphalt path on the south side of the road — the Little Traverse Wheelway — is heavily used by bicyclists and in-line skaters.) Or for closer contact with the water, go left (north) to the rip rap retaining wall and follow it right (east)

across a series of grassy areas and parking lots.

At 0.4 miles the route passes a creek that spills out from near the top of a limestone bluff on the right (south), drops 20 feet, spills and splashes over rock terraces, turns sharply past a large willow, flows under a footbridge, then disappears under Bayfront Drive and sneaks out from under the rip-rap to join the bay. The picturesque falls is the site of countless prom and wedding photos and even an occasional wedding itself. A few yards to the left (east), a 60-step stairtower scales the vertical face of the cliff 35 feet up to Sunset Park, with panoramic, elevated views of the bay.

Cross over here to the Wheelway, on the south side of Bayfront Drive, and continue straight (east) in front of Sunset Park. For 50 yards on the right, directly below the park, the face of the limestone bluff — exposed by the former quarry operations — edges the path, with close-up looks at the fossilized, sedimentary remains of tropical saltwater seas that submerged Michigan some 350 million years ago.

At the east end of the cliff, also on the right, is another quarry remnant, a former lime-kiln pond, now a lagoon. About 175 yards farther, at the east end of the large pond, the route turns right (south) and drops on steps to a bridge across a shallow channel that drains the lagoon's overflow into a tiny wetland area, edged by willows, grapes, and cherries and filled with reeds, cattails, and often ducks.

The blacktop path then serpentines east 225 yards through a new arboretum, whose many small, grassy knolls are spiked with several different species each of young pines, maples, willows, hawthorns, birches, aspens, oaks, and shrubs — none of which, however, are marked with any kind of identifying label.

At about ¾ mile, the arboretum path reaches a stairway up to US-31 just past a small, dark-brown DPW pumphouse. Turn left (north) here and follow a gravel road that angles 100 yards northeast to rejoin the Wheelway. Follow the Wheelway right (east), temporarily losing sight of the bay as the route passes trees and residences on the left, then curves between houses and Oleson's shopping center, on the right. (The current bare, block back of the center is scheduled to be painted with a mural.) Two blocks later, the route reaches a sidewalk on the north side of US-31.

The route follows the sidewalk for 225 yards, crosses Boulder Lane, then veers left (north) and drops to a cedar hedge at the edge of a bluff 25 feet above the bay. The route bears right (east) 125 yards along the hedge to its end, then follows an open grassy plateau — with whiplash views between the bay, on the left, and Bay View's Victorian summer homes, perched above US-31 on the right — another 275 yards to the turn-around point, a pedestrian overpass into the heart of the architecturally and historically unique summer community. (For details about Bay View, see pgs. 30-39.)

PERRY HOTEL
TO WINTER SPORTS PARK

A widely varied route that begins near one of the city's finest outdoor dining spots; takes in elevated views of the marina area, the bay, and the Winter Sports Park; makes a dry run down a ski/sled slope; and encounters a sometimes-above-ground, sometimes-underground stream.

LOOP TRAIL 1.6 MILES

ALLOW 1 HOUR

Facilities: Restrooms are located in the lower lobby of the Perry Hotel, a water fountain is available at Arlington Park, and restrooms and concession stands are open at the Winter Sports Park during park operating hours.

Directions: From the junction of US-31 and US-131, drive north then east on north US-31 0.7 miles to a traffic signal at Lake Street (the second signal after crossing the Mitchell Street Bridge and curving left, north). Or from the junction of M-119 and US-31, drive west on south US-31 2.6 miles to the traffic light at Lake, (the next light after passing a softball field, on the right).

Turn east onto Lake and go two blocks to Howard Street. Turn left (north) onto Howard and go one block to Bay Street. Turn right (east) onto Bay and go one block to Lewis St., at the corner of the Perry Hotel. Go east a few yards farther to a parking lot on the right (south), next to (west of) the Emmet County jail and sheriff's department.

From the parking area walk west down Bay Street about 60 yards, then cross over to the guests-only parking area on the west side of the city's first brick hotel — the conspicuous, cream-colored Perry, built in 1899. (For more details, see p. 110.) The route heads north (toward the bay) through the lot. About ⅔ of the way across, stone steps on the right (east) rise to the beautifully landscaped Veranda, a covered and open outdoor dining area with unobstructed, elevated views that sweep from the marina breakwater to the Nub's Nob moraine (p. x).

From the steps the route continues north to Rose Street, then turns right (east) onto a sidewalk that runs a half block past the Veranda's rough, shaped-concrete-block retaining wall, then the hotel, to Lewis Street. Across Lewis straight ahead is Penn Plaza, an office complex that occupies a former railroad station constructed at the turn of the century on the site of the city's first train depot, built in 1875 and destroyed by fire in 1899.

The route turns left (north), crosses Rose, and follows a sidewalk between a sturdy iron and stone fence, on the left, and replica globed gaslights, on the right. The 125-yard walkway edges the city's most-recent waterfront-area reclamation and beautification project, an eyesore former quarry that in year 2000 was filled in, seeded with grass, and studded with a few young trees. Elevated, open views here sweep from the large swale over the marina area to the bay.

At the end of the sidewalk and lights, the route turns right (east) across Lewis, then turns left (northeast) to follow a sidewalk along grassy, open Arlington Park, on the right (south). A community garden there marks the site of the former Arlington Hotel, the largest and most elegant of the city's more than 20 turn-of-the-century summer hotels, all of which but the Perry ultimately burned or were torn down or converted to other uses. The star-shaped educational garden area comprises eight cells divided by brick walkways. Each of the distinctly varied plots is planted and maintained by a different non-profit group, with guidance from MSU-trained Master Gardeners.

The route follows the sidewalk 125 yards to its end, then crosses a grassy strip 35 yards to Winter Park Lane, at ⅓ mile. There the route turns right (southeast) and rises a half block up Winter Park Lane to the intersection with Arlington and Grand avenues. The route crosses Arlington and turns left (east) onto a sidewalk on the south side of the road, which gradually curves and rises 200 yards to its highest point, with open views of the bay from about 60 feet above.

Just a few feet farther, the sidewalk is interrupted by a 15-yard stretch of grass, followed by a final 25-yard strip of concrete. Where the sidewalk ends, the route crosses over to a wide gravel and grass shoulder on the north side of Arlington, then drops 325 yards yards to Lafayette Street, at 0.7miles.

Turn right (south) and follow Lafayette, which rises moderately 225 yards to a junction with Beaubien. The rising route continues straight (south) 30 yards then winds east and again south 100 yards to a 90-degree bend left (east) into a parking area behind Traverse Woods apartments. There the route continues straight (south) onto a two-track-wide, sandy path through a beech/maple forest.

The trail-road follows a valley between two high moraines as it rises moderately 100 yards to a 90-degree bend left (east), at one mile. On the left (east) there, a 3-foot section of corrugated metal culvert sticks out from under the path behind a large maple and ash. Directly across the trail from the culvert, the route turns right (south) onto a narrower path that heads between a pair of widely spaced birch up the face of a moraine to the top of the Winter Sports Park's northmost downhill ski/sled run. The climb can seem near vertical, rising about 50 feet over only 50 yards.

The route then drops 50 vertical feet down the 125-yard-long ski run to the foot of the rope-tow area, where a small, wood-topped, mesh-sided box encloses a tiny waterfall that is part of one of the area's most unusual water bodies. The ¾-mile-long, unnamed creek originates at a small wetland ¼ mile south near Petoskey High School (p. 18), dives and jogs under Mitchell Street, briefly re-emerges, and then is routed through a large concrete tube under the sports complex's soccer field to the box. There the creek free-falls 10 feet to another concrete pipe, which carries the water north under the parking lot. Runoff from the ski hills is also channeled into the large, open hole under the box, adding to the flow.

From just north of the parking lot the stream makes its longest appearance, closely following Winter Park Lane (p. 26) ¼ mile to Arlington Avenue. The creek then crosses beneath the street, breaks out again to meander about 50 yards through Arlington Park, dives under US-31, and bursts out of a limestone cliff as a picturesque 20-foot waterfall (p. 21). From there, the creek spills and splashes over rock terraces and flows under a footbridge and then a waterfront road before making its final disappearance into the bay

From the winter-park drain box, the route heads northwest 40 yards to, then drops gently about 100 yards across the parking lot to a junction where three roads — two paved and one gravel — fan out. Turn sharply left (south) onto Rose Street, which a block later turns sharply right (west) and, for 175 yards, runs between the creek, about 40 yards away on the right,

and a bluff that rises steeply through maples to Bay Street, on the left.

Rose then angles away from the creek and rises steeply 125 yards through a residential area to a high point, just before the junction with Williams Street. A formidable residence on the right, there, is fronted by a pair of Greek Revival porticos — one, a large, two-story, four-columned structure and the second, a smaller one-story, two-column entryway. Kitty-corner across Rose is an equally large and grand vintage dwelling. The white, shingle-sided, 2½-story residence includes a round, window-wrapped turret that juts out from a bay-side corner.

From Williams, Rose drops steeply 150 yards to a T junction at Arlington. Turn left (south) onto Arlington, which becomes Division Street, and go a block to Bay. Turn right (west) onto Bay and go a block to the starting point parking area.

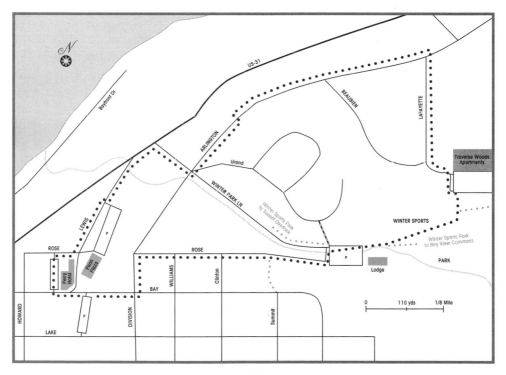

Winter Sports Park to Sunset Overlook

An easy stroll along a small creek, followed by a rigorous rise rewarded by the finest up-high, year-round perspective of the bay from anywhere in the city.

LOOP TRAIL 0.7 MILES
ALLOW 1 HOUR

Facilities: Restrooms and concession stands are open at the Winter Sports Park during park operating hours.

Directions: From the junction of US-31 and US-131 go north, then east on north US-31 1.2 miles to Winter Park Lane, marked by a large, brown "Winter Sports Park" sign. Or from the junction of US-31 and M-119 go west on south US-31 2.1 miles to Winter Park Lane. Turn south onto Winter Park Lane and go one bock to a 5-way intersection (all streets have stop signs). Continue straight (south) on Winter Park Lane 0.3 miles to the sports area's parking lot.

Head to the northwest (bay) side of the parking lot, dropping gently to a junction where three roads — two paved and one gravel — fan out. Continue straight (northwest) on the gently rising middle road — asphalt, tree-lined Winter Park Lane. Fifty yards from the road junction, on the left, a creek that has been piped underneath the complex's soccer field and parking lot breaks free and flows in the open along the lane to ultimately drop over a limestone cliff at Sunset Park (p. 21) before joining the bay. (For more details on this unique sometimes-above-ground, sometimes-underground stream, see p. 24).

About 50 yards farther, as you approach the crest of the brief rise, in view on the left down through a thick growth of maple, Box Elder, and underbrush are the mostly intact remains of a small, old concrete dam. About 40 yards farther, as the road begins to drop, the sounds made by the moving water become perceptibly louder.

Seventy-five yards farther, on the left as the lane enters a residential area, a quaint, covered pedestrian bridge connects one of the homes to its parking area across the stream.

The lane then levels out and, 250 yards farther, reaches a junction with Arlington and Grand avenues and, just a block straight ahead, US-31. Turn very sharply

right (southeast) onto Grand, twisting back to parallel Winter Park Lane while rising 175 steep yards to a junction with Fairview. Turn left (northeast) onto Fairview and go 125 moderately steep yards past residences to where the road makes a 90-degree turn right (southeast).

Off the road to the left there is a large, grassy walkers' turnout with sweeping views of the bay (p. *x*) over the treetops but also framed by a few towering maples.

The route then rises another 75 yards to the high point, a second grassy area at the edge and crest of a bluff at Fairview and Sunset, at 0.5 miles. One-of-a-kind bird's-eye views from 160 feet above and only ¼ mile from the bay sweep from the bluff's steep face out over US-31, which winds gently through Bay View, to a full-frontal panorama of the state park dunes.

The route then drops southwest on Sunset 150 yards to Grand, turns left

(southeast) onto Grand, and rises moderately 100 yards to a junction with a gravel road (where asphalt Grand curves left, rises, and ends a few yards farther at a cul de sac).

Turn right (south) onto the gravel road, which drops steeply 125 yards to the Winter Sports Park parking area.

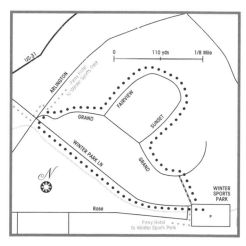

27

WINTER SPORTS PARK TO BAY VIEW COMMONS

> *A rigorous, varied route that starts at an underground stream, briefly follows the shore of a prehistoric Great Lake, passes an abandoned artesian water-supply system, cuts through a mature beech/maple forest, then circles the core of one of the nation's most-unique summer communities.*

Evelyn Hall

ROUND TRIP INCLUDING THE 0.4-MILE LOOP AROUND THE COMMONS, 2.8 MILES

ALLOW 1½ HOURS

Facilities: Restrooms and concession stands are open at the Winter Sports Park during park operating hours. Public restrooms are also located in the lower level of Bay View's Wade Administration Building.

Directions: From the junction of US-31 and US-131 go north, then east on north US-31 1.2 miles to Winter Park Lane, marked by a large, brown "Winter Sports Park" sign. Or from the junction of US-31 and M-119 go west on south US-31 2.1 miles to Winter Park Lane. Turn south onto Winter Park Lane and go one bock to a 5-way intersection (all streets have stop signs). Continue straight (south) on Winter Park Lane 0.4 miles to the sports area's parking lot.

From the south edge of the parking area, head 40 yards southeast, east side of the lodge over a small berm to a small, wood-topped, mesh-sided box covering a tiny waterfall that is part of one of the area's most unusual water bodies. The ¾-mile-long, unnamed creek originates at a wetland ¼ mile south near Petoskey High School (p. 18), dives and jogs under Mitchell Street, briefly re-emerges and then is routed through a large concrete tube under the sports complex's soccer field to the box. There the creek free-falls 10 feet to another concrete pipe, which carries the water north under the parking lot. Runoff from the skiing/sledding hills is also channeled into the large, open hole under the box, adding to the flow.

The stream then makes its longest appearance beginning just north of the parking lot, from where it closely follows Winter Park Lane (p. 26) a ¼ mile to Arlington Avenue. The creek then crosses beneath the avenue, breaks out again to meander about 50 yards through Arlington Park, dives under US-31, and bursts out of a limestone cliff as a picturesque 20-foot waterfall (p. 21). From there, the creek spills and splashes over rock terraces, flows under a footbridge and then a waterfront road before making its final disappearance into the bay

From the waterfall box, continue southeast just a few feet to the base of the ski hill's rope-tow, then climb 70 feet over 175 yards on the steep, sandy, shady rope-tow corridor cut through pines.

From the top of the hill the trail continues straight (east) 25 yards on a narrow, well-worn path through a few pines. (The wide path left along a wood fence leads to the top of skiing/sledding runs.) Continue straight (east) across a 50-yard-wide, open,

grassy area (passing through an open metal gate at the south end of a wood fence that bisects the area) to Bay View Avenue.

The route turns left (north) and follows the street — with views over the treetops to Harbor Springs (p. *xii*) — 100 yards to the asphalt's end at the edge of a private residence. The route follows the property line 30 yards north then 30 yards east at the top of a steep bluff whose edge marks the shoreline of a prehistoric Great Lake.

As the last of mile-thick Ice Age glaciers receded from the upper Midwest some 11,000 years ago, they temporarily (in geologic time) blocked drainage of melting water to the east through the present-day St. Lawrence Lowland. The mammoth ice dam created a single large lake, named Algonquin, that flooded much of the present-day Great Lakes area to the height of this bluff. Michigan's Upper and Lower peninsulas were separated by a broad, deep strait that covered most of Emmet, Cheboygan, and Presque Isle counties. Only the peaks of the highest glacial

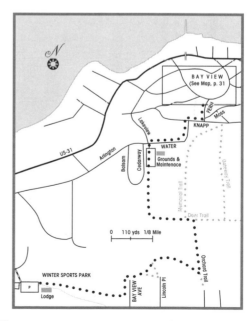

29

moraines — such as the Boyne Highlands and Nub's Nob "mountains" (p. *xiii*) — poked out of the water as islands. When further ice retreat plus "rebound" raising of the land from the glaciers' tremendous weight finally exposed the St. Lawrence, the lake level dropped.

From the bluff's edge behind the residence, the well-worn trail bears left (northeast) into the woods toward a pine tree posted with a "No bikes" sign. From the pine, the trail drops gently, then moderately through mature beech and maple down the face of the bluff (past a faint trail that forks right at 50 yards) 150 yards to a fork.

Bear left (north), continuing to drop, now steeply, 125 yards to near the bluff's base. From there the trail levels out as it curves east then southeast around the head of a sapling-studded, wildflower- and reed-filled meadow, on the left (north), to meet Bay View Woods nature area's Orchard Trail.

About ⅔ of the way across that 100-yard stretch and visible about 15 yards off the trail to the left (north) is a 6-foot-long, 4-foot-wide, 2-foot-high concrete box. The meadow here, though steeply sloped and well-drained, is kept perpetually wet by some of the many springs that flow throughout Bay View Woods, and this cistern was used decades ago to collect the artesian flows and pipe them to Bay View.

Turn left (north) onto Orchard Trail, which drops gently between the meadow, on the left (west), and a large ridge, on the right (east). Another clear perspective of the small cistern, about 20 yards off the trail to the left (west), comes about 25 yards after passing between a pair of posts.

About 150 yards past the posts, Orchard Trail reaches a rest bench at the junction with Deer Trail. Turn left (west) and

follow the wide path through magnificent beeches and maples 25 yards to the junction with Memorial Trail (p. 13), which branches off right (north). Continue straight (west), passing — just steps later and almost in the middle of the trail — an exposed 40-foot section of the iron pipe that once carried spring water from the cistern above.

A few yards farther, at 0.7 miles, the trail meets a 50-yard section of boardwalk that immediately makes a 90-degree bend right (north) then edges a lowland, on the right (west), that is filling in with 20-foot-tall Red Ash and other saplings. From the walkway's end the path runs 150 yards past Forget-Me-Nots to a wood pedestrian-access-only gate at Bay View's Buildings, Grounds and Maintenance complex.

Continue straight (north) 100 yards on a gravel then asphalt service road at the west edge of the complex to Water Street. Turn right (east) onto Water, which gently curves 300 yards then, at one mile, turns left (north) and runs another 70 yards straight to its end at Knapp. Turn right (east) onto Knapp and walk one block (about 100 yards) to Fern. Turn left (north) onto Fern, wind 140 yards to Encampment, then cross the street to a new administration building for Michigan's most-historic and uniquely beautiful summer community, Bay View.

Begun by Michigan Methodists in 1875 as a religious Chautauqua-type summer retreat, the Bay View Association today comprises 441 mostly Victorian summer residences (p. 34) spaced along winding, tree-lined streets that follow a series of natural terraces overlooking the bay. All are so beautifully and accurately maintained that the entire community is on the National Register of Historic Places and has been designated a National Historic Landmark.

During the first season, several hundred Bay View members slept in tents and listened to spiritual lectures while sitting on benches lined up the hillside south of a set-aside area called Tabernacle Park. Over the following years, several buildings were constructed around the perimeter of that central "commons" area, now shaded by magnificent towering beeches and maples. Most structures were built before 1900. A few are plain and practical, most are are fine examples of Victorian architecture, and a few are singularly grand and ornately beautiful.

All were erected to further the association's goals of providing communal opportunities for spiritual, intellectual and cultural growth in an atmosphere of rest, respite and relaxation. And not exclusively for association members. Most of Bay View's educational classes, concerts, theatre productions, lecture series, and other programs have long been open to the public.

Thanks to an eight-year restoration program completed in 2000, the Commons buildings have been restored as nearly as possible to their original state. All but the library and Hall Auditorium have rust-red asphalt-shingled roofs. Most are painted white with dark-green trim, colors that were popular in resort areas during the 1920s.

Walk to the west side of the Wade Administration Building, turn right (north), drop down a few steps, and then follow the sidewalk between the Wade Building and Evelyn Hall.

The largest and most-colorful Queen Anne structure in the Commons, Evelyn

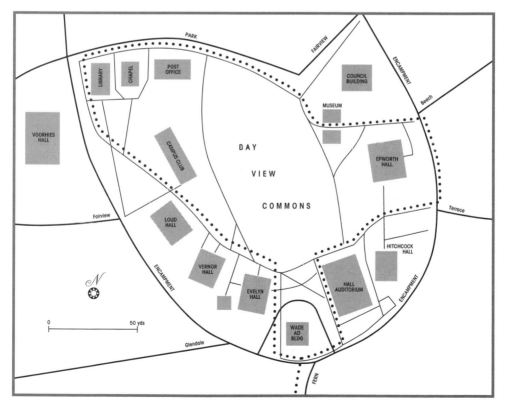

Hall is also considered to be one of the *country's* finest examples of what is called Steamboat Victorian architecture. The three-story stunning structure is a complex, controlled explosion of turrets, porches, balustrades, shiplap and shaped-shingle siding, dormers, leaded and stained glass, decorative arches, and a protruding two-story gazebo. Completed in 1890 at a cost of $4,500, the building was the summer headquarters of the Woman's Christian Temperance Union for 28 years. Today, the upper floors house a theater costume work room and studio practice areas for gifted musicians who attend a small, select summer music school here.

Where the sidewalk reaches a T junction, turn left (west) in front of Evelyn Hall and proceed a few yards to Vernor Hall. (The barn-shaped building set back between Evelyn and Vernor halls is a private cottage.)

From its opening in 1897, blocky, somewhat austere (by Bay View standards) Vernor Hall has been used by the Association's Music Department. In fact the building was originally simply called the Music Hall until renamed in 1967 in honor of Dr. F. Dudleigh Vernor, Bay View's organist from 1912 until 1962.

From Vernor Hall the sidewalk gradually curves right (north), passing between Loud Hall, on the left, and the Campus Club, on the right.

Loud Hall is one of many Commons buildings that are asymmetrical, that is they are designed and built to look different from every perspective. The angular lines of large, beautiful Loud Hall are softened somewhat by small overhangs that arc up over the first-level roofs of a pair of 2½-story wings that jut out slightly on opposite sides of a 3½-story center section. The

structure's multiple gables have different finish treatments, including latticework, shaped shingles, and sunburst patterns. Built in 1887, the building has always been used for education, including currently serving as a site for adult education seminars.

The Campus Club has been the center for both indoor and outdoor games and other activities since 1919. Croquet lawns, shuffleboard courts, and expansive lawn-bowling rinks back the long, narrow ranch-style building, completed in 1952 and expanded south in 1979.

From here, take the sidewalk that angles northwest about a block to the front of the orange-brick library building. When constructed in 1931, this English-cottage-style structure incorporated two unique, lasting features. Three vertical bands of brick step in from chimneys on each end to attach them to the exterior walls. And the unusual pattern and color of the slate roof is said to be repeated on only one other building in the country. During the May to October summer season (residents are not allowed to use their cottages the remainder of the year), members typically check out some 3,200 of the facility's 8,500 volumes.

West across Encampment Avenue from the library is Voorhies Hall, a 1950s elementary-school-style building with a small theater used for lectures, plays, operas, and movies.

Take the sidewalk around the front of the library to Park Avenue, turn right (east), and follow the sidewalk from the library a few feet to a structural schizophrenic. The building was a grocery store from the 1890s to the 1960s, when it was turned into a children's Craft House. In 1993 the structure was converted to a chapel, but the north facade was restored to its 1899 appearance. A look through the "grocery store" window focuses not on canned goods, but an altar. The small chapel is used for weddings, baptisms, and memorial services. Large Sunday worship services are held at Hall Auditorium.

Immediately next door to the east is Bay View's post office, flanked on each side by tiny real estate offices. Bay View members own their cottages but lease the land from the Association. Though some cottages here have been in families for six generations, others are sold, often by word of mouth but also by the two brokers here. Prospective buyers do not have to be Methodist but must be approved by a screening committee.

Take the sidewalk, curving generally east from the post office, passing by lawn-bowling courts, about two blocks toward a pair of small Pagoda-style buildings on the right, then take the sidewalk between them. The board-and-batten-sided building on the right was built in 1876 as the association's first public building, known as the Speakers Stand. The building to left was constructed in 1880 and for many years operated as a bookstore selling Methodist publications. Next to the side walk between the structures is the first fire hydrant installed in Bay View, around 1883. Both buildings currently house a museum with limited hours.

To the left (northeast) behind the museum is the Council Building, constructed in 1886 and used since 1924 as the site for weekly women's groups meetings and programs.

The sidewalk from between the museum buildings leads east to Epworth Hall, another beautiful, asymmetrical structure that appears to have been constructed by stacking three stories worth of differently shaped and sized porches. Interrupting the west wall are four closely spaced, stepped windows that likely follow and illuminate an interior staircase. This building was erected in less than three months during 1891 at a cost of $3,000 paid for with pennies saved by the Epworth League, a Methodist youth organization. Married Bay View music faculty members have used the hall as a summer residence since 1938.

Continue east on the sidewalk to its end at Encampment Avenue, turn right (south), and take the street (there is no sidewalk here) in front of Epworth Hall a few yards to a sidewalk that heads right (west) toward Hitchcock Hall.

Three-story Hitchcock Hall, originally built in 1889 as a headquarters for Bible study, now houses Bay View Conservatory of Music practice rooms. Its rectangular, steep-roofed northeast corner is reminiful of a three-story stockade blockhouse whose lower level is wrapped in a porch skirt.

Just steps to the west is the 2,000-seat John M. Hall Auditorium, not only Bay View's most-imposing edifice, but also the most-dramatic departure from the Victorian preponderance. The large, sturdy, stark white Greek Revival concrete box was completed in 1915 at a cost of $50,000. A quartet of two-story cylindrical columns help form a wide portico, and doors and windows around the back (south) third feature hundreds of small, pastel-colored plastic panes hand-cut and hand-installed by a Bay View couple 20-25 years ago.

Pass in front of the auditorium, turn left (south) along its west wall, follow the sidewalk and steps back up to Encampment and Fern, and retrace your steps back to Winter Sports Park.

Bay View Cottage Stroll

Michigan's most-historic and uniquely beautiful summer community had humble beginnings. In 1875 Michigan Methodists formed an association that purchased 338 acres and organized a religious summer-camp meeting here. The 500-600 "seekers" who attended that first session spent six days listening to sermons and talks while sitting on wood benches set in a newly cleared area overlooking the bay. At night they slept in tents that surrounded the preaching area.

Just two years later, streets, parks, and other public areas had been platted, and about 20 cottages had been built. And by the turn of the century, most of the community's 441 summer places plus some two dozen "commons" buildings were in place. (For details about those structures, see pgs. 31-33)

The association's activity list also grew to include Chautauqua-type communal opportunities for not just spiritual, but also intellectual and cultural growth plus recreation. And not just for the benefit of members. Many of the association's Summer Assembly Programs — which include a variety of educational classes, concerts, theatre productions, and lecture series — have long been open to the public.

Since almost all of the "cottages" — which range from cabin to mansion size — were built during the last years of the Victorian Era, most were designed in the Victorian architectural style. That is, features were picked from the buffet of previous architectural styles and combined, often to achieve as much ornamentation as possible. The degree of elaboration here is unrelated to size and ranges from subtle expressions to bric-a-brac explosions.

Interspersed from the opposite end of the architectural spectrum are some comparatively plain, blocky, hip-roofed minimalist structures.

But overall the community is an extravaganza of turrets, dormers, pillars, porches, ballisters, bargeboard, gingerbread trim, lattice and spindle work, patterned-clapboard and shaped-shingle siding, and steeply pitched roofs with decorative gables. Most structures are beautifully preserved or restored, with color schemes ranging from the plain, white and green-trimmed 1920s resort look to a variety of multicolored eye-catchers.

Bay View has also maintained such historical integrity that the entire community was placed on the National Register of Historic Places in 1972. To preserve that status, that same year an architectural review board was formed to oversee all structural changes. In 1987 the community was also designated a National Historic Landmark.

The cottages are closely spaced along a labyrinth of winding, tree-lined streets that traverse and connect a series of natural terraces rising to nearly 200 feet above the bay. So this stroll has lots of ups and downs as it passes almost half of Bay View's cottages, including several of the most architecturally and historically unique or significant plus a few pre control-committee anomalies.

Because Bay view residents are only allowed to occupy their cottages from May 1 to October 31 (most places are shuttered or boarded up during the off-season), best time to take this stroll is from about May 15 to October 15.

LOOP TRAIL 2½ MILES

ALLOW 1½ HOURS

Facilities: Public restrooms are located in the lower level of the Wade Administration Building.

Directions: From the junction of US-31 and US-131 go north, then east on north US-31 1.6 miles to a traffic light at McDonald Drive and the entrance to Oleson's Shopping Center. Or from the junction of US-31 and M-119 go west on south US-31 1.8 miles to the same intersection.

Turn south onto McDonald and go a half block to Arlington Avenue. Turn left (east) onto Arlington and wind ¼ mile to a stop sign just past the entrance to Bay View. Continue straight (east), now on Water Street, and follow Water 3 blocks as it curves north to a stop sign at Knapp Avenue. Turn right (east) onto Knapp and go one block (about 100 yards) to Fern Avenue. Turn left (north) onto Fern, which winds 140 yards to parking spots along Encampment Avenue in front of the Wade Administration Building.

From the administration building, head west on Encampment Avenue about 60 yards to a fork at Glendale Avenue. Continue straight (west) on Glendale 125 yards yards to the austere, white, three-story Terrace Inn, on the right (north). Forty-three Victorian decorated guest-rooms in this step-back-in-time, bed-and-breakfast country inn, open since 1911, come with private baths but no phones or TVs. Walk up onto the inn's porch and pass through the lobby — paneled in hemlock and furnished with the inn's original, now-antique oak furniture. Leave (north) out onto the front veranda and drop on concrete steps and a sidewalk to Fairview Avenue.

Turn left (west) and go 50 yards to a 2¾-story, gray, white-and-black-trimmed home that sprawls back at 1536 Fairview (1), on the left (south). The huge (reportedly the largest in the community, in terms of usable interior space) but otherwise unassuming home was originally owned by the sister of colorful, former Louisiana Governor Huey "Kingfish" Long, and is still in the family.

Continue west along Fairview, which curves northwest to an intersection with Lakeview and Park avenues. On the northeast corner there, at 1505 Park, is the "Butterfield" cottage (2), built in 1879. Unique to this otherwise modest, minimalist-style, nearly square, white-with-green-trim

house is a bracketed, covered, railed porch that wraps completely around. A tiny second-story balcony is centered atop the porch on the south side.

Head southwest along Lakeview, which rises moderately 150 yards to an intersection with Glendale and a grouping of three of the largest dwellings to be found away from the front-row, bay-view streets. A white, 2¾-story Victorian home (3) two lots (30 yards) west on Glendale is front-centered by a shingle-sided octagonal turret, with steeply-pitched roofs covering rectangular wings that spoke out from it. A pair of piggy-back covered porches angle out from the northwest corner toward the bay. The cottage is also asymmetric — that is no sides are the same — and so reveals a different appearance with each changing curbside perspective.

Next door to the east, on the southwest corner, is a formidable, gray and white, two-story minimalist-style home (4) whose large hip roof is interrupted by a pair of small dormers. A sizeable portion of the upper level is built out over a lower-level porch that wraps the front and part of the east side.

East across Lakeview and nearly filling one of Bay View's largest lots is an imposing, white and blue-gray, two-story Victorian home (5) with octagonal turrets punctuating each end of a large pitch-roofed box that has multiple smaller pitch-roofed wings fanning and layering out behind. A covered, railed porch that wraps around half the lower level is topped by a pair of smaller porches poking out on the second level.

Go east along Glendale 150 yards to a fork at Knapp Avenue. Bear right (southeast) onto Knapp and gently rise 200 yards to Water, at 0.6 miles.

Turn right (south) and descend along

Water 60 yards to Bay View's only rustic-style cottage (**6**), a tiny log cabin on the left (east) that overlooks a small creek.

Backtrack up to Knapp, turn right (east), and walk 50 yards to what may be the only alpine-, chalet-looking cottage in the community, at 1690 Knapp (**7**). Exposed above the porch at the front of the white A-frame structure are large trusses, beams and braces.

Continue east along Knapp another 50 yards to the junction with Fern Avenue, at ¾ mile. Turn left (north) onto Fern, then 25 yards farther bear right (northeast) onto Moss Avenue and go 275 yards (passing Cedar Street, Swift Field, and then a Tot Lot, all on the right) to the Octagon Cottage (**8**), at 1859 Moss. Built in 1910, the yellow, green-trimmed, cupola-topped, two-story, eight-sided structure (the only such-shaped cottage in Bay View) is nearly wrapped with a pillared but rail-less veranda.

Continue east along Moss 75 yards (past Highland Avenue, on the right) to a junction with Forest and Buffet. Turn sharply left (north) and follow Forest,

which curves and drops 60 yards to Terrace Avenue, at one mile. Turn right (east) and walk along Terrace 75 yards to a fork at Hemlock Street. Continue straight (east), rising and winding gently on Terrace another 125 yards to what may be the most-daring paint scheme in the community (**9**) — deep-gray and bright-crimson Ohio State colors that cover an otherwise relatively modest cottage up on the right (south).

Continue east along Terrace 175 yards to an intersection with Forest Avenue and narrow Preston Avenue. Dominating the southeast corner there is large, long, white Ruth Crist Hall, a two-story former hotel now used as a dormitory for select students attending Bay View's prestigious summer music school.

Across Terrace just a few steps from the east end of Crist Hall is Bay View's only Cape Cod-looking structure (**10**), a small, quaint three-dormered cottage sided with weathered-dark cedar shingles set off by white windows and shutters.

Backtrack 75 yards along Terrace to the intersection with Forest and Preston. Turn

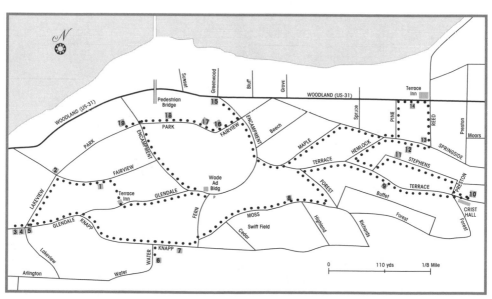

right (north) onto one-lane Preston, which drops 30 yards to Stephens Lane. Turn left (west) onto the narrow alley, which rises 100 yards to the backside of a two-story, century-old cottage, on the right (north) at 1979 Stephens (also 608 Springside) (11). Protruding from a corner of its back porch is a half-gazebo topped with a "witch's-hat" roof.

Continue west on Stephens, which drops 25 yards then rises steeply as it curves south 100 yards to Terrace. Turn right (west) and follow Terrace 60 yards to Hemlock, at 1½ miles. Turn sharply right (northeast) onto a sidewalk that descends along Hemlock 100 yards to stairs that

drop to Springside Avenue.

Turn right (east) and follow Springside 50 yards to the yellow-brown, cream-trimmed Waite Cottage (12), up on the right. Different-sized three-quarter circles that make up facades between the columns of its decoratively latticed, two-story front porch give this otherwise-simple A-frame cottage, built in 1887, a distinctly Moorish look.

A cottage across the street 25 yards farther east, at the northwest corner of Springside and Reed Avenue(13), stands out for two reasons. Forest-green shutters brightly painted with colorful, ribbon-tied floral arrangements border all windows of

the two-story home plus decorate what may be the only remaining (but no longer used for its original purpose) outhouse in Bay View.

Head north on Reed one block to Woodland Avenue across from Terrace Inn, a hotel that has operated continuously since 1887. Turn left (west) and follow Woodland 40 yards to a large, plain, two-story, gray home at 1976 Woodland (14). Local lore has it that in the early 1930s author Margaret Mitchell finished writing *Gone With the Wind* here, but evidently secretly since none of her biographies mention trips to Michigan.

Continue west on Woodland 25 yards to Pine Street. Turn left (south) and follow Pine one block to Springside, at 1.8 miles. Turn right (west) and follow Springside 100 yards (past Spruce, on the right) to the junction with Maple Street, on the left. Turn left (southwest) and follow Maple, which rises 175 yards to Terrace. Turn right (west), follow Terrace 60 yards to Encampment, then turn right (north) and follow Encampment 125 yards to Fairview.

Continue on Encampment another 40 yards down to the most obviously elaborate summer home in Bay View (15), on the left (west) near the corner of Woodland. The two-story asymmetrical dwelling, built in 1877, is sided with differently shaped shiplap boards placed in a variety of patterns. Half-circle arches connect the ballisters of a covered porch that wraps the front of the lower level. Open exterior stairs climb from a smaller second-story porch into an open tower topped with a bell-shaped roof. And board-cut sea serpents crawl across the peaks of a trio of opposing pitched roofs with differently decorated gables. A teal, lavender, and cream color scheme beautifully highlight all architectural features.

Backtrack up Encampment to Fairview, then bear right (southwest) along Fairview 50 yards to the junction with Park Avenue. To the right (north) on the corner at 1715 Fairview is a gray cottage (16), built in 1881 and still trimmed with the original, unique, crest-patterned window surrounds. Original, elaborately decorative, white bargeboard also finishes the ends of multiple cross gables plus a center octagonal turret.

A yellow home 50 yards west at 1695 Park (17) is reportedly the second largest, in terms of interior space, in Bay View and was formerly used as a bed and breakfast.

Fifty yards farther west at 1665 Park (18), is a small, off-white-stucco, light-teal-trimmed cottage where, during the summers of 1919 and 1920, author Ernest Hemingway regularly partied with Luman Ramsdell, like Hemingway a WWI vet and whose physician father, Oscar, was Petoskey's first automobile owner (p. 116).

Continue west about 150 yards along Park, across Encampment, to Bay View's only private brick building, on the right (north) at 1595 Park (19). The original cottage on this site burned and this replacement was constructed years before the current architectural controls were in place.

Backtrack east 50 yards along Park to Encampment, turn right (south), and follow Encampment, which curves and rises 275 yards back to the administration building.

BAY VIEW FITNESS TRAIL

An opportunity for an all-around outdoor workout while viewing Victorian architecture along the sinuous streets of the state's most-historic and uniquely beautiful summer community.

Twenty varied fitness stations range in difficulty from simple stretches to more-rigorous routines that require strength, balance and agility. Signs at each station show and tell what to do. Equipment is sized for both children and adults, and repetition numbers are recommended for both those just beginning a fitness program and those already in shape.

All stations except numbers 6, 7, and 15-19 are on the right-hand side along the route.

LOOP TRAIL 1 MILE

ALLOW 45 MINUTES IF YOU DON'T EXERCISE; 1½ HOURS IF YOU DO

Facilities: None.

Directions: From the junction of US-31 and US-131 go north, then east on north US-31 1.6 miles to a traffic light at McDonald Drive and the entrance to Oleson's Shopping Center. Or from the junction of US-31 and M-119 go west on south US-31 1.8 miles to the same intersection.

Turn south onto McDonald and go a half block to Arlington Avenue. Turn left (east) onto Arlington and wind ¼ mile to a stop sign just past the entrance to Bay View. Continue straight (east), now on Water Street, and follow Water 3 blocks as it curves north to a stop sign at Knapp Avenue. Turn right (east) onto Knapp and go 0.2 miles to Bay View's Crafts Pavilion Center, on the left. A few informal, dirt parking spots are available off a turnaround area here, plus off-road parking along Knapp is permitted.

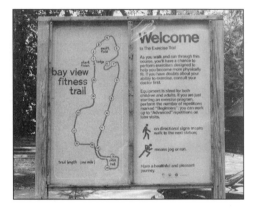

Walk west along Knapp about 10 yards to Station #1, an arm-swing warm-up.

Continue west along Knapp about 35 yards to station #2, toe touches.

Continue west along Knapp 20 yards, then curve right (north) onto one-lane Cedar Street, along the west edge of Swift Field, another 30 yards to station #3, shallow knee bends with toe rises.

Continue north on Cedar 75 yards farther to station #4, waist stretches.

Continue north 10 yards to Moss Avenue, turn right (east) and follow along the north edge of Swift Field 75 yards to station #5, another toe-touch variant.

Continue east along Moss 60 yards to the east edge of Swift Field, just before the Tot Lot building, where a black arrow points the way right (south) 25 yards to station #6, a deep stretch performed by standing with legs apart and arms overhead and then bending to touch the ground.

Continue south, along the west side of a row of large pines 25 yards to their end. There, make a U-turn left around to the other (east) side of the trees and follow them north 35 yards to station #7, a second arm-swing variant.

Continue north 15 yards back to Moss, turn right (east) and go 60 yards, past the Tot Lot on the right, to the Octagon House (p. 37), on the left at 1859 Moss. Twenty yards farther at station #8, classic chin-up bars are tucked into a small grove of balsam fir at the southwest corner of Moss and Highland avenues.

Continue east on Moss 25 yards farther to its end at the junction with Forest Avenue and Bufett Lane. Bear right (continuing east) along Forest 75 yards to the junction with Richards. Ten yards farther east on Forest is station #9, a bar vault consisting of a 4 x 6 timber that angles up from about 15 to 30 inches over an 18-foot span. Instructions direct you to side vault over the bar at a comfortable height then return underneath, also at a comfortable height.

Continue east along Forest 75 yards to station #10, a bar that you are instructed to grip and then, while keeping your legs straight, lift them to a horizontal position and hold for a count of three.

Continue east along Forest 100 yards to a second junction with Bufett Lane. There, south across Forest is station #11, a variation of situps in which you sit on a raised log and — with feet held by hooking them under another raised, but lower log — repetitively bend your torso backward and forward.

Continue east along Forest 50 yards (just past a trail that heads into the Bay View Woods nature area, on the right) to station #12, where several 6 x 6's of varying heights have been sunk vertically into the ground. Instructions direct you to step up alternately with your right and left leg to the top of one of the posts.

About 15 yards farther, where a gravel road heads off to the right, continue following Forest as it curves left (north) to station #13 (a simple side stretch), behind (south of) large, white Ruth Crist Hall, about 25 yards before Forest ends at Terrace Avenue.

Though an arrow points north, proceed 20 yards east behind Crist Hall to station

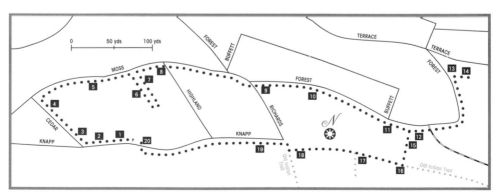

#14, a sideways jump back and forth over a 14-foot-long log, one end on the ground, the other raised about a foot.

Backtrack south up Forest, then turn sharply west and go just a few feet past station #12 to a black arrow that points left (south) onto a trail into Bay View Woods nature area. Turn left (south) onto the trail and immediately on the left is station #15, a jump up to and stretch-hang from one of a pair of raised bars.

Continue south on the wide trail through imposing beeches and maples, rising moderately then steeply 60 yards to meet the Old Indian Trail (p. 48), at station #16, which involves repetitively lifting one of three different-size and -weight logs from the ground over your head.

Turn right (west) onto the Old Indian Trail and follow the wide path 50 yards to station #17, a variant of classic pushups in which feet are placed on one of three bars at different heights.

Over the next 100 yards, the root-webbed trail then drops quickly and briefly, levels out, then again drops steeply to station #18, a standing, sideways leg lift.

Just a few yards farther west the trail reaches a T junction with a wide, wood-chip-covered path. Turn right (north) and walk 40 yards, through the Old Indian trailhead gate, to the corner of Richards and Knapp. Turn left (west) and follow Knapp 35 yards to station #19, a combination toe touch/knee bend/arm swing.

Continue west along Knapp 150 yards back to the Crafts Pavilion Center and station #20, an 18-foot walk on a nearly Z-shaped balance beam.

MEMORIAL TRAIL

A near-level, woodchip- and leaf-cushioned path through imposing maple, beech, and hemlock and past rocky reminders of the Ice Age. The lowland forest floor in this section of the Bay View Woods nature area is also mounded with hundreds of hillocks — dirt-covered, decayed root remains of previous generations of toppled trees.

LOOP TRAIL ¾ MILES

ALLOW 30 MINUTES

Facilities: Rest benches along the trail.

Directions: From the junction of US-31 and US-131 go north, then east on north US-31 1.6 miles to a traffic light at McDonald Drive and the entrance to Oleson's Shopping Center. Or from the junction of US-31 and M-119 go west on south US-31 1.8 miles to the same intersection.

Turn south onto McDonald and go a half block to Arlington Avenue. Turn left (east) onto Arlington and wind ¼ mile to a stop sign just past the entrance to Bay View. Continue straight (east), now on Water Street, and follow Water 3 blocks as it curves north to a stop sign at Knapp. Turn right (east) onto Knapp and go 1½ blocks (just past Fern Avenue) to an inconspicuous two-car parking area, on the right (south).

For additional details about this route — with excellent listings and descriptions of lichens, mosses, ferns, wildflowers, and other vegetation that grows here — pick up a 20-page interpretive brochure from a box at the trailhead and return it when done with the walk.

Immediately south of the trailhead, a footbridge crosses a creek that drains the Old Indian Trail swamp (p. 48) and other area lowlands. Forty yards farther, the myrtle-lined path reaches the junction with Gateway Trail (p. 46). Just a few feet off the trail to the left (east) there, the huge roots of a 60-foot-tall Sugar Maple embrace a large granite boulder with an attached small brass plaque honoring William Gilbert, "who worked to preserve and interpret these woods for future generations."

Turn sharply right (west), paralleling the creek, which separates the trail from Bay View cottages along Knapp Street. Twenty-five yards farther, an inconspicuous side trail, edged with small tree limbs, leads right (north) to a simple wood creekside memorial to Harold E. Kohn.

Twenty yards farther (at interpretive marker #2), about 10 yards off the trail to the right (north), stands a stately hemlock that took root a century ago in the rotting stump of another tree. The "nurse" stump has since completely decayed, leaving the top couple of feet of the huge hemlock's extensive root system exposed. Throughout the area, several other hemlocks as well as Yellow Birch perch on similar root stilts.

At the left edge of the trail 50 yards farther (at marker #4) is a Sugar Maple with a burl about five feet up its trunk, just above a fork. If this tree stood in a harvestable forest, the distinctive, swirled-grain pattern of its wartlike scar might be turned into bowls, artwork or veneer. Many other maples (and a distinctive birch; see p. 49) throughout the woods here are also burled.

Fifteen yards farther (just past marker #5) the route passes, on the left, another nurse-stump hemlock — this one a 30-inch-diameter, 70-foot-tall specimen with a tunnel passing beneath its trunk between exposed root tentacles.

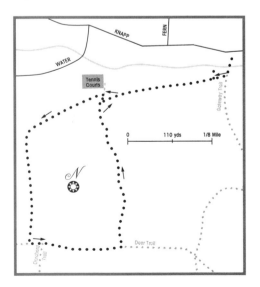

On the left 50 yards farther is the first of many granite boulders scattered along both sides of the trail. The rocks were likely plucked out of northern Canada by advancing glaciers some 20,000 years ago, carried several hundred miles south over several thousand years, and dropped here when the mile-thick ice sheet melted. On the left 75 yards farther (at marker #8) is another "glacial erratic," as geologists term the immigrant stones. This medicine-ball-size specimen is covered with lichens that, by secreting acids over eons, will eventually break this rock down into soil. Other kinds of lichens (plus liverworts and mosses) do the same to dead trees, only much quicker.

At 0.2 miles the path reaches a T junction. Turn sharply right (northwest) onto an unnamed trail toward tennis courts visible on the right. Thirty yards farther the trail forks again. Bear sharply left (southwest) onto the narrower path where, on the right about 15 yards farther, a ½-ton glacial erratic displays plainly visible grooves and gouges created by the rasping, grinding action of the powerful glacier that transported it.

At 0.3 miles the trail turns left (south) and follows the east edge of a sapling-filled lowland 75 yards to a T junction. Turn left (east) and go 30 yards, gradually rising to a junction with Deer and Orchard trails. Continue straight (east) on Deer and slightly rise 100 yards — at the base of a bluff, on the right, and beneath towering maples, hemlocks, and a few beech — to the junction with Memorial Trail. Turn left (north) onto Memorial and curve 200 yards to a fork. Take the right fork, now backtracking east 300 yards to the intersection with Gateway Trail. There, turn left (north) and return 50 yards to the trailhead.

Gateway/Algonquin Trails

A perpetually shaded probe of the quiet far reaches of Bay View Woods nature area. Start and finish is near-level walking beneath the canopies of magnificent lowland maples and beech, with a climb to and drop from the shore of a prehistoric greater-than-Great Lake in between. An added plus: specimens of Basswood, Black and White Ash, Trembling (Quaking) Aspen, Yellow and White Birch, Sugar Maple, Eastern Hemlock, White Cedar, and American Beech are labeled along the Gateway section of the route.

LOOP TRAIL 1.4 MILES
ALLOW 1 HOUR

Facilities: Rest benches along the trail.

Directions: From the junction of US-31 and US-131 go north, then east on north US-31 1.6 miles to a traffic light at McDonald Drive and the entrance to Oleson's Shopping Center. Or from the junction of US-31 and M-119 go west on south US-31 1.8 miles to the same intersection.

Turn south onto McDonald and go a half block to Arlington Avenue. Turn left (east) onto Arlington and wind ¼ mile to a stop sign just past the entrance to Bay View. Continue straight (east), now on Water Street, and follow Water 3 blocks as it curves north to a stop sign at Knapp Avenue. Turn right (east) onto Knapp and go 1½ blocks (just past Fern) to an inconspicuous two-car parking area, on the right (south).

For additional details about this route — with excellent listings and descriptions of lichens, mosses, ferns, wildflowers and other vegetation that grows here — pick up a 20-page interpretive brochure from a box at the trailhead and return it when done with the walk.

Immediately south of the trailhead, a footbridge crosses a creek that drains the Old Indian Trail swamp (p. 48) and other area lowlands. Forty yards farther, the myrtle (periwinkle)-lined path reaches the junction with Memorial Trail (p. 43). Con-

45

tinue straight (south) along Gateway past a Sugar Maple — at the right (west) edge of the trail 50 yards farther — with a large burl about seven feet up its 15-inch-diameter trunk. The obvious, abnormal growth is likely the result of a long-ago injury, and beneath the bark of the knobby protrusion is a distinctive swirled-grain pattern highly prized by artisans and artists.

At the trail's edge on the left (east) just 15 yards farther (interpretive marker #2), is a Yellow Birch, identifiable by its yellowish-gray, horizontally peeling, curling bark. Seedlings of this species often establish themselves in rotting logs, stumps, and even moss on rocks. This tree, for instance, sprouted out of a stump that has now almost completely decayed, leaving the birch perched on thick strands of exposed roots (photo, below).

Throughout the area, several other birch as well as many hemlocks grow from

such "nurse" stumps.

At ⅛ mile (at marker #4), the winding and gradually rising trail forks; bear right (southwest). A hundred yards farther, another burled maple pokes out of the myrtle next to the trail on the right (north).

At about ¼ mile the wide, gradually curving route reaches the junction of Gateway, Algonquin, and Deer trails. Continue straight (south) on Algonquin, which rises moderately and steadily as it skirts a small spring-fed wetland on the left then, at ⅓ mile, turns sharply left (east) at marker #2. (Another trail here continues straight (south) up the steep face of a high bluff, ending at private property off Mitchell Street.)

The main trail rubs the head of the narrow wetland and weaves through a valley created by the bases of several small to large bluffs, hills, and ridges (past a second side trail south) to marker #3, at 0.4 miles. From there the trail rises briefly, but steeply, climbing 50 feet in 75 yards to the top of a bluff, where a post is engraved with "congratulations." A remnant sign on the post's opposite (east) side warned bicyclists (bikes are no longer allowed on Bay View Woods trails) headed the opposite way to "gear down."

For the next quarter mile the trail is near level as it winds along the bluff's edge from where, 10,000 years ago, you could have dipped your toes in a post-glacial Great Lake. As the last of mile-thick Ice Age glaciers receded from the upper Midwest, they temporarily (in geologic time) blocked drainage of melting water to the east through the present-day St. Lawrence Lowland. The mammoth ice dam created a single large lake, named Algonquin, that flooded much of the present-day Great Lakes area to the height of this bluff.

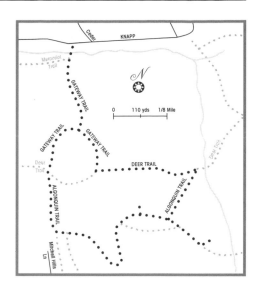

Michigan's Upper and Lower peninsulas were separated by a broad, deep strait that covered most of Emmet, Cheboygan, and Presque Isle counties. Only the peaks of the highest glacial moraines — such as the Boyne Highlands and Nub's Nob "mountains" (see p. *xiii*) — poked out of the water as islands. When further ice retreat plus "rebound" raising of the land from the glaciers' tremendous weight finally exposed the St. Lawrence, the lake level dropped.

At ½ mile the route passes a wide trail that loops off to the right (southeast) and 75 yards farther, at marker #6, reaches the junction with a well-worn trail that leads left (north) a few yards to a dramatic barricaded view 75 feet down the near-sheer face of the bluff. During the summer, a few square inches of Little Traverse Bay are visible in the distance through the thick foliage. During leafless seasons the view improves but is still obstructed by limbs and trunks. Also then, you get a clear look at Deer Trail, which runs across the valley floor in front of the bluff.

The main trail continues generally east another 100 yards to a fork, at marker #10. Continue straight (east) 125 yards through maples studded with a few beech and huge White and Yellow Birch (past the other junction with the wide south-side loop trail) to a junction with a wide two-track road, at marker #11 and 0.7 miles. Bear sharply left (north) onto the narrow footpath, which drops past a towering, moribund birch 75 yards to a second barricaded overlook, this one at the edge of a 25-foot-deep, 40-foot-wide ravine carved out of the hillside by erosion. Most of the time the area is dry, but following heavy rains, washout volumes of runoff water from flatland areas south of the ridge rush through and continually enlarge the gully.

Return to the main trail, backtrack 100 yards west, and turn right (north) onto a well-worn trail (at marker #10) that drops 200 steep yards to the junction with Deer Trail, at a lowland area.

Head left (west) along Deer Trail, which follows the base of the bluff on the left (south) and the lowland on the right (south). Seventy-five yards from the junction, the wide, level trail passes under a birch deadfall and 200 yards farther (at marker #6) edges a large field of shiny, leathery-leaved myrtle (periwinkle) that spills down from the base of the bluff.

Seventy-five yards farther the route rejoins the Gateway Trail. Turn right (south) onto Gateway and descend gradually 125 yards to a fork, at 1¼ miles. Continue straight, on the right fork, and return 225 yards to the trailhead.

OLD INDIAN TRAIL

This strand in a web of Bay View Woods nature-area trails traverses a glacially deposited ridge, crosses over natural springs, and cuts through the heart of a beautiful cedar/hemlock swamp.

LOOP TRAIL 0.9 MILES
ALLOW 45 MINUTES

Facilities: Rest benches along the trail.

Directions: From the junction of US-31 and US-131 go north, then east on north US-31 1.6 miles to a traffic light at McDonald Drive and the entrance to Oleson's Shopping Center. Or from the junction of US-31 and M-119 go west on south US-31 1.8 miles to the same intersection.

Turn south onto McDonald and go a half block to Arlington Avenue. Turn left (east) onto Arlington and wind ¼ mile to a stop sign just past the entrance to Bay View. Continue straight (east), now on Water Street, and follow Water 3 blocks as it curves north to a stop sign at Knapp Avenue. Turn right (east) onto Knapp and go 0.3 miles to a two-car parking area, on the right (south) where Knapp dead-ends at Richards.

For additional details about this route — with excellent listings and descriptions of lichens, mosses, ferns, wildflowers, and other vegetation that grows here — pick up a 20-page interpretive brochure from a box at the trailhead and return (recycle) it when done with the walk.

Twenty-five yards south of the trailhead, just before reaching a boardwalk, turn sharply left (east) onto a wide, root-webbed path that rises moderately beneath towering hemlocks and beech to follow the crest of a long, narrow moraine created by retreating glaciers some 12,000 years ago. This steep-sided ridge was likely formed when till — tons of earthen debris carried by the ice from Canada — washed into space between two large glacier snouts or perhaps even huge pieces of ice that had broken off from the main sheet. When the snouts or blocks of ice themselves melted later, they left the molded depressions on either side of this ridge. The large, low area on the right (south) is now a cedar/hemlock swamp. The smaller, elongated gully on the left (north) rises quickly on the opposite side to a few of the backmost of Bay View's 441 cottages.

Edging the soft trail in the first 50 yards are several skinny Striped Maples, characterized by their oversize 3-lobed leaves and smooth, greenish-white, vertically striped bark. Some here reach 15-20 feet in height, uncommon because as a favorite deer food, the understory shrub doesn't typically survive to grow much past 2-4-feet. (Striped Maples are particularly easy to spot in fall when their hand-size leaves turn to a unique creamy-yellow color.) And over the first 200 yards the route also encounters three of 20 stations that make up the Bay View Fitness Trail (p. 40).

At ¼ mile the path drops steeply and quickly, brushes the shoulder of Division Road, and turns sharply right (south), around the cattail-filled east end of the swamp. A few yards farther, a short boardwalk leads through a small but thick stand of cedar.

From the end of the boardwalk the trail rises gradually into a second-growth beech/maple forest, where it again turns sharply to head southwest, following the base of a steep, 30- to 50-foot-high bluff on the left and still skirting the swamp on the right. Spread beneath the hardwoods are the almost completely rotted stumps of hemlock and cedar that were clear-cut decades ago.

At just past 0.4 miles, the route crosses two short boardwalks. At the end of the second, 15 feet off the trail to the right (north), the base of the trunk of a yellow birch is wrapped with an unusually large burl. The massive growth of injury-induced scar tissue has, over decades, formed a likeness of a tree-climbing sea tortoise (see photo, left).

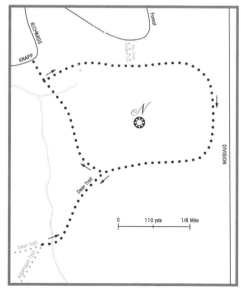

Thirty yards farther the route reaches the east terminus of Deer Trail. Just a few yards farther, at ½ mile, the trail reaches another boardwalk at one of the area's few relatively open spots, where several brooks weep from the hillside and meander down into the swamp. The first (eastmost) of the shallow, slow-moving flows is usually wide enough to provide a treadmill for Water Striders, insects whose long, hair-thin, hair-covered legs allow them to literally walk on water. Almost touching the 150-yard-long boardwalk on the right about halfway across is a still-living, good-size cedar riddled with deep, elliptical holes drilled by woodpeckers.

The level boardwalk ends at a golf-cart-size granite boulder, likely a northern Canadian immigrant picked up by advancing glaciers some 20,000 years ago, carried several hundred miles south over several

thousand years, and dropped here when the ice melted.

The trail then rises briefly but steeply 20 yards on root-webbed dirt to another section of boardwalk that brushes a pair of uniquely shaped trees, a beech and a hemlock on the left at interpretive marker #3. During the trees' formative years, the weight of eroding surface soil slip-sliding down from the steep hillside above bent their slim, supple trunks to near horizontal. As the pair matured, they again straightened up, deforming their posture into a J-shape.

From there the boardwalk drops, then steps down as it winds right (west) through small to large beds of Forget-Me-Nots, whose tiny, pale-blue and white blossoms mat the forest floor spring through fall. The walkway bottoms out at a rivulet created by springs plus runoff from flatlands far above.

The boardwalk then rises 20 yards and ends at the junction with the Algonquin Trail, at 0.6 miles. Turn around here and backtrack the 250 yards to the junction with the Old Indian Trail. There, turn left (north) and follow the wide, woodchip-covered path 50 yards to a scenic section of boardwalk that snakes 200 yards through the swamp to meet the chip-covered path that leads 50 yards back to the trailhead. Representatives of some of the half-dozen varieties of ferns that grow in the area line the pressure-treated planks and occasionally poke up through them. And the picturesque stretch also passes through natural arches formed by uprooted, canted cedar and hemlock.

Tannery Creek
to Bay View

A mostly open walk with sustained, sweeping views of the bay plus close encounters with samples from one of the nation's finest collections of Victorian architecture.

ROUND TRIP 2.3 MILES

ALLOW 1½ HOURS

Facilities: Glens is a large, full-service grocery
store with restrooms for use by their customers. Plans call for the construction of a
scenic overlook of the bay at the foot of
Rice Street. Fine dining plus restrooms for
restaurant patrons and hotel guests are
available at Stafford's Bay View Inn.

Directions: From the junction of M-119 and
US-31, go west on south US-31 0.35 miles
to Rice Street, one block west of the traffic
signal at the entrance to Glens Shopping
Plaza. Turn right (north) onto Rice and
drive two blocks to where it dead-ends at
Shire. Turn right (east) into the plaza parking area, then immediately bear left down
to a wide gravel parking area that edges
the bay. Park at the extreme east end of the
lot.

From the gravel parking lot, step a few
feet north onto the Little Traverse Wheelway. Just a few yards east of the east end of
the lot, Tannery Creek spills its final 50
yards around and over windfalls before
joining the big water.

The route follows the blacktopped
Wheelway west. On the right (north)
about 60 yards past the west edge of the
parking lot, is a unique "mushroom-style"
house patterned after two dozen such
structures built in Charlevoix from 1925
to 1955. The characteristic style — with
smooth, irregular curves replacing most
straight lines — was created by Charlevoix
nonarchitect Earl Young, who used local
materials such as limestone, fieldstone, and
shipwreck timber to construct his cottages.
Topped by wavy cedar-shake roofs, the
dwellings, including this one, resemble
huge toadstools that have naturally sprouted from the earth.

About 125 yards later the route leaves
the Wheelway, turning right (north, under
utility lines) onto Kent Street, which dead-
ends 125 yards later at Edgewater. Turn left
(west) onto Edgewater, which hugs the bay
— with nice views (p. *x*), particularly east
to the state-park area — for about 100
yards before ending at Hampton. Turn left
(south) onto Hampton, go 75 yards to

Newberry, turn right (west), and go about 140 yards to a T junction with Division, which marks the east edge of one of the nation's most unique summer communities — Bay View.

Begun by Michigan Methodists in 1875 as a religious Chautauqua-type summer retreat, the Bay View Association today comprises 441 mostly Victorian summer residences plus some two dozen "commons" buildings spaced along tree-lined, winding streets that follow a series of natural terraces overlooking the bay. Some of the summer homes are plain and practical, most are are fine examples of Victorian architecture, and a few are singularly grand and ornately beautiful. All are so beautifully and accurately maintained that the entire community is on the National Register of Historic Places and has been designated a National Historic Landmark. (For further details about Bay View see pgs. 30-39.)

Turn right (north) onto Division, which quickly sweeps left (west) onto Bayside. For the next 0.2 miles the narrow, blacktop road gently winds between Bay View cottages on the left (south) and continuous panoramic views of the bay, just feet over the rocky shore to the right (north).

In sight in the distance ahead is a 25-foot-high rip-rap retaining wall fronting a bluff that curves for a quarter mile to the route's turnaround point at Bay View's breakwater and Recreation Club/Boathouse area. About 100 yards before ending at Reed Avenue, Bayside closely follows a 4-foot-high rip-rap wall, on the right, that protects the roadway from erosion.

At Reed the route turns left (south) and moderately rises 40 yards to the north edge of parking areas for Stafford's Bay View Inn, a hotel that has operated continuously since 1887.

The route turns right (west), along the left (south) side of a small, lush memorial garden, where cremains of Bay View residents have been mixed with the soil. From the west edge of the garden the route continues straight (west) on a grassy, 25-yard-wide former railroad bed, again between Bay View cottages on the left (south) and continuous panoramic views of the bay over the high bluff's edge, to the right (north). (Though this former railroad bed is commonly viewed and used as a public right of way, it is owned by the Bay View Association, which could restrict access to members only. Bay View has not done that, and so it is important to respect this private property and adjacent residents' privacy so that the route remains accessible.)

At one mile — in view through an opening to the left (south) down Greenwood Avenue (about 75 yards before

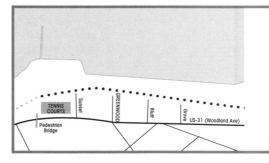

reaching tennis courts) — is what may be Bay View's most beautifully maintained and colored home. The ginger-bread-trimmed showcase, built in 1877, is a teal-, lavender-, and cream-colored explosion of ballistered porches, towers, patterned shiplap siding, gables, and opposing pitched roofs topped with board-cut sea serpents.

The route continues west 275 yards, past the tennis courts, to the turnaround point, a metal pedestrian bridge across US-31.

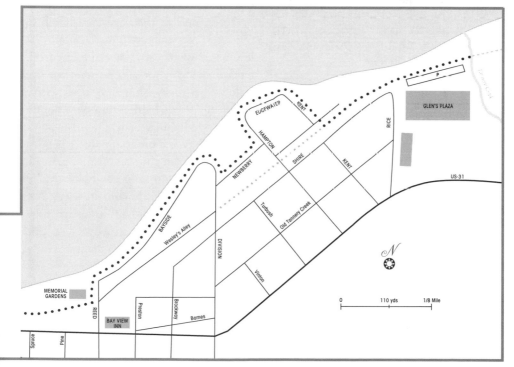

TANNERY CREEK CONNECTOR

A near dead-level strip of asphalt that can be walked on its own or used to connect to and lengthen, as desired, several other walkabouts. A loop trip is also possible, a 3¼-mile route on the connector path to the state park entrance road, down the road to the beach, and along the beach back to Tannery Creek.

DISTANCE TO STATE PARK BEACH BOUNDARY 275 YARDS

DISTANCE TO PORTAGE TRAIL AT TANNERY CREEK CAMPGROUND 0.4 MILES

DISTANCE TO SPRING LAKE PARK 0.6 MILES

DISTANCE TO PETOSKEY STATE PARK ENTRANCE ROAD 1.6 MILES

DISTANCE TO OLD BALDY AND PORTAGE TRAILHEADS 2 MILES

DISTANCE TO BEACH COMB AND DUNE INTERPRETIVE TRAILHEADS 2.1 MILES

LOOP TRAIL TO AND THROUGH STATE PARK WITH RETURN SOUTH ALONG THE BEACH 3¼ MILES

Facilities: Glens is a large, full-service grocery store with restrooms for use by their customers. Restrooms and water are available at Spring Lake Park. Toski Sands Plaza includes a full-line grocery store plus a convenience store. Facilities in the state park include picnic areas, two modern campgrounds, and a beach area with bathhouse (including restrooms), a children's playground and concession area.

Directions: From the junction of M-119 and US-31, go west on south US-31 0.35 miles to Rice Street, one block west of the traffic signal at the entrance to Glens Shopping Plaza. Turn right (north) onto Rice and drive 2 blocks to where it dead-ends at Shire. Turn right (east) into the plaza parking area, then immediately bear left down to a wide gravel parking area that edges the bay.

From the gravel parking lot, step a few feet north onto the Little Traverse Wheelway, an asphalt pathway that currently runs from just north of Petoskey State Park 12 miles south and west to Bay Shore. Plans call for the route to ultimately link Charlevoix to Harbor Springs.

Follow the Wheelway to about 25 yards east of the parking lot, where Tannery Creek spills its final 50 yards around and over windfalls to join the big water.

To connect to the State Park Beach (p. 69), cross over the creek, turn left, and follow a well-worn path down the east creekbank to the bay shore. Turn right (east) and follow the rocky shoreline as it curves about 200 yards to the state park boundary, marked by the concrete remnants of an old pier. Stay as close to the water as possible, especially in the section that passes in front of a condominium complex. Michigan law says that, though the state owns the land under the bay's ordinary highwater mark, the property owner *controls* any and all exposed land to the water's edge and may prevent the public from trespassing. Condominium owners have not yet done that, and so it is important to respect this private property so that it remains accessible. Should it ever be posted, however, it would be legal and not considered to be trespassing to walk in the water through this section.

And walking in the water is one of the best ways to search for Petoskey stones, which can be abundant in this section. The official state rock is actually petrified coral that lived in a salt-water sea that covered Michigan 350 million years ago. The fossil's characteristic gray-green, white-bordered, hexagonal markings can best be seen when wet, so successful hunters dodge waves at the water's edge, wade out into shallow areas, and even search shores in the rain. Spring ice-out and major fall storms wash in fresh specimens, which range from thumbnail- to boulder-size.

From Tannery Creek, the paved Wheelway continues east through an open right-of-way that fronts a row of condominiums. Near the east end of the row, a trail branches off left (north) to Petoskey State Park's Tannery Creek Campground, where access is blocked by a chain-link fence. Seventy-five yards farther, at the east end of the row, a 225-yard-long trail branches off left (north) and passes through the fence to the campground road. A hundred fifty yards north down the road it is possible to connect to the Portage Trail by walking a pathway north from behind a restroom/concession building.

The Wheelway continues straight (east) on a former railroad bed to the shoulder of M-119, at 0.4 miles. At M-119 where the Wheelway veers left (north), it is possible to carefully cross the busy highway to Spring Lake Park and the trailhead to the Round Lake outlet (p. 56).

The Wheelway continues north, closely skirting thick growths of ash, young basswood, an occasional elm, and several shaggy-barked Hop-hornbeam. Across the highway at 0.8 miles is the former Petoskey Brewery, which from the 1890s to 1925

produced Petoskey Sparkle Beer and Petoskey Export. A few yards farther the Wheelway passes in front of Joie de Vie French and European antiques.

For the next ¾ mile, a near-continuous strip of office, commercial, residential, and light-industrial development separates the pathway from the state park dunes' backsides, whose height and steepness is further hidden by heavy tree growth. Even the near-vertical rear of Old Baldy (p. 62) — the park's highest dune, which rises 170 feet behind the middle of the Circuit Control Corporation (CCC) complex, at 1.3 miles directly across from the north end of Toski Sands Plaza — is barely discernable in summer.

At 1.6 miles the pathway reaches the Petoskey State Park entrance road. To walk to the Old Baldy, Portage Trail, Beachcomb, and Dune Interpretive walk trailheads, follow the driving directions (from the park entrance) for those walks. To connect with the Round Lake Nature Preserve, see page 72.

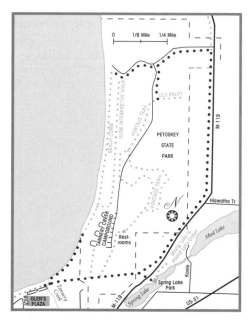

SPRING LAKE
TO ROUND LAKE OUTLET

A near-level walk past Spring, Mud, and Round lakes, with especially nice views across Round. Start and finish is at Bear Creek Township's showcase park.

Spring Lake Park

ROUND TRIP 3.2 MILES

ALLOW 2 HOURS

Facilities: Facilities at Spring Lake Park include a unique picnic pavilion/observation platform tiered out over the water plus restrooms and water.

Directions: From the junction of US-31 and M-119, go north on M-119 0.3 miles to the Spring Lake Park entrance, at the south end of park.

Before heading out on the main route, walk the woodchip-covered path that loops 25 yards around a natural mini-arboretum at the water's edge off the south end of the parking area. Growing nearly trunk-to-trunk in just a 1,500-square-foot area are a surprising number and variety of trees and shrubs, including Northern White Cedar, Red and White Ash, a lone White Birch, Box Elder, a 20-foot-tall Pin Cherry and, at the southwest corner, a small colony of Balsam Poplar, an aspen-family member whose sap's fragrance is similar to that of the evergreen Balsam Fir.

The route to Round Lake begins at the pavilion. Plans call for the construction of 1,500 feet of boardwalk that will head northeast, skirting the Spring Lake shore and crossing over the wetland at the north end. Until that project has been completed, walk to the northwest corner of the parking area, climb to the wide shoulder and grassy median of M-119, head north a few yards to a yellow "bike path" sign, then veer right, along an abandoned railroad bed to Konle Road, at 0.2 miles.

Cross Konle and continue on the railroad bed, passing between the former Petoskey Brewery on the left (p. 54) and Mud Lake, on the right. The small lake is a textbook example of the efficient, orderly, natural process that ultimately fills in all lakes, ponds, and other contained water bodies. The water body fills with runoff sediment and then with vegetation that grows, dies, falls to the bottom, and produces peat until the depression is so full that surface water no longer stands in it. The time it takes depends on the size and depth of the water body and whether there are feeder streams or underground springs.

Cattails, rushes and other aquatic plants grow first, fronted quickly by Water Lilies, Duckweed, and other floating plants. When their decayed remains creates enough peat to become solid around the edges, water-loving shrubs, then trees such as Tamarack and willow take over, which forces the aquatic plants farther out into the water.

These concentric rings of vegetation types also tend to make the remains of the original water body round, no matter its original shape. At oblong Mud Lake, the largest growth of vegetation is on the north and south (elongated) ends, gradually reshaping the open water to a circle. (The same is true at long, narrow Spring Lake.) When outer rings have encroached to the point that there's no longer enough water to support the aquatic plants, Mud Lake will officially become a swamp then, eventually, dry land. (Even-closer looks and more-detailed explanations of this type of habitat should come at the north end of Spring Lake when the boardwalk is built and interpretive signs are installed.)

At a half mile, the pathway crosses paved Hiawatha Trail, then briefly skirts, on the left, a willow- and ash-filled wetland formed through the drainage area from Mud Lake to Round Lake. Hiawatha Trail immediately angles left (northeast), and the route from here parallels that road 15-20 yards from it, buffered from it by heavy growth of a variety of trees. And except for one gradual bend, the remaining one-plus mile of the route is rail straight, level and, except at high noon, shady.

At 0.7 miles, glimpses of Round Lake come through dense underbrush, and 100 yards farther, a well-worn path leads left through the growth 15 yards down to the shore and interesting views across the water. The white air-supported roof of Griffin (ice) Arena, for instance, resembles a pillow thrown onto the treetops. Farther right, ski runs at Nub's Nob form wide treeless gashes down the east face of one of the area's highest "mountains," a near-1,300-foot-high pile of earthen debris deposited by glaciers.

For the next ⅓ mile the lake disappears from view as the predominantly aspen-lined trail passes through an area that in spring is thick with thousands of flitting, harmless dragonflies. The water then reappears, this time through strips of yards between several shoreline residences.

About halfway down that 100-yard stretch, the trail passes an old "Round Lake, Elevation 602' " sign. In theory then, Round Lake should drain west the short ¾ mile to Little Traverse Bay, whose level is

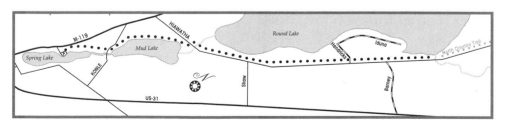

more than 20 feet lower. And it did 5,000 years ago when much-deeper waters covered the area. But over the next two millennia the level of those pre-Great lakes dropped, exposing their sandy former bottoms to consistent west winds. Over time the Petoskey State Park dunes formed and plugged Round Lake's route to the bay.

Now the lake's outlet (at this walk's turnaround point) flows east to Crooked Lake and ultimately through several other major lakes and rivers to Lake Huron, more than 40 miles away. That entire waterway was used for centuries by American Indians and, later, French explorers, but the Round to Crooked lakes section is no longer navigable due to road development. The remainder of the route is now the recreationally used Inland Waterway.

Two hundred fifty yards past the Round Lake sign, at 1¼ miles, the trail crosses gravel Hendricks Street. Two hundred yards farther, as the trail passes a couple of houses on the left, the turnaround point — marked by a curve in the trail — comes into view and less than ¼ mile farther is reached.

There, at the Round Lake outlet, the trail nearly touches the sand-bottomed lake. Views across the clear, shallow, blue-green water include a unique perspective of the back side of the imposing state-park dunes (photo, below). A well-worn path that continues north a few yards inland from a long, narrow strip of white-sand beach is on private property.

A small but prominent point to the left (southwest) less than ¼ mile across the water and marked by a pair of tall pines (photo, below) was once an outdoor theatre where — for several years beginning in 1905 and produced by the GR & I Railroad — the play *Hiawatha* was performed by native Ojibway Indians.

(Note: Most of the trail from Spring Lake to here has followed the North Country Trail (NCT), which when completed will run continuously from the Appalachian Trail in Maine 3,200 miles to the Lewis and Clark Trail in North Dakota. From this point at Round Lake, the NCT continues northeast along the railroad bed to Conway, then turns north to Wilderness State Park.).

Round Lake

PORTAGE TRAIL

> *A varied walk along the forested floor of a broad interdunal valley, through a glacier-sculpted labyrinth, past the remains of a tannery "hairpit," and up to panoramas from the crests of high dunes.*

LOOP TRAIL 1.6 MILES
ALLOW 1-1/2 HOURS

Facilities: Water fountain across from the boulders that mark the trailhead. Facilities elsewhere in the park include picnic areas, two modern campgrounds, and a beach area with bathhouse (including restrooms), a children's playground and concession area.

Directions: From the junction of M-119 and US-31 go north on M-119 1-1/2 miles to the entrance to Petoskey State Park. Turn left (west) onto the entrance road and go 300 yards to the contact station (daily or annual vehicle permit required for entry). Continue straight another 300 yards to a fork. Turn sharply left (south) and go 250 yards to the camper registration building area. Just before reaching the building, bear left (east) into a parking area loop.

From the parking loop, head southwest to the Dunes Campground entrance road, then follow it west a few yards past a small woodlot, on the left, and through yellow gates to an intersecting one-lane, north-south paved road. Turn left (south) onto the road, following signs and markers to lots 36-70 and gradually winding right (west) to two large boulders on the left (south) between lots 57 and 59. The sidewalk-wide trail heads left (south) between the rocks and into a quarter-mile-wide, densely forested lowland between huge, high, parabolic-shaped dunes on the east (not visible because of heavy tree growth) and their lower flat foredune ridge to the west. (For further information about these dunes and their formation, see Dune Interpretive Walk, p. 64.)

Seventy-five yards in, the sandy, level trail reaches the junction with a well-worn path from the left (northeast) that connects back to the Dunes Campground's eastmost lots and the road to Tannery Creek Campground.

Twenty-five yards farther, at ¼ mile, the path reaches an intersection. The trail left (northeast) again connects to the campground lots and road. Take the side trail to the right (west), rising moderately 100 yards beneath oak, pine and cedar to nice views of the bay (p. *x*) from the crest of the dune ridge, 30 feet above the water.

Backtrack to the main trail, turn right,

and continue south — paralleling the Tannery Creek Campground road 25-75 yards from it — 100 yards to a fork. Bear left (east) onto a trail that leads to the campground road. Cross over the asphalt and, on the other (east) side, take a well-worn path that plunges into a thick stand of mature hemlock that — likely because the trees were too young at the time — escaped harvesting when a nearby tannery clear-cut most of the area, beginning in 1886.

The deeply shaded path gradually loops right (from east to south) and gently to steeply rises as it weaves through a maze formed by hundreds of small to large glacier-sculpted ridges, bluffs, gullies and ravines. Little vegetation grows on the forest floor here, except where the sun peeks through the foliage in areas of oak and, later, beech that interrupt the dense hemlock. (When leaves blanket the ground in late fall, the trail here can be difficult to discern.) And though the trail here skirts the base of a 75-foot-high dune, the trees also block

views of the large, high sand mountain.

At ¾ mile the trail breaks out of the hemlock darkness, rises and falls steeply over a sandy ridge, then passes through pine, oak and aspen out to an open area at the edge of a ¼-mile long, 150-yard-wide sandy depression. The empty, dry oval bowl is a former "hairpit" — a settling basin enclosed by 30-foot earthen dikes — to which the nearby tannery (p. 70) pumped its animal and other waste products for a few years during the late 1940s.

The trail bears right (west) across the north end of the dried-up lagoon then gently rises and falls over loose sand through oak and pine 150 yards to a fork. (The wide path left follows a valley between two low moraines 200 yards south to a restroom building, with pay phones and soft-drink vending machine.) Take the trail to the right, which rises and falls gently to moderately as it twists north, then west, then drops quickly to the campground road, at one mile. The route crosses the road and, 75 yards farther, reaches a T junction.

Turn sharply right (north) onto the wide trail that parallels the campground road 25-75 yards from it. (The path left leads south to Tannery Creek Campground.) A hundred yards farther, a side trail branches off right (east) to the road, and 75 yards past that junction a second trail also branches off to the road. About 20 yards farther, the main trail passes between a pair of 60-foot-tall, 2-foot-diameter white pines, the first on the left and the second a few steps farther on the right.

Just 10 yards farther, at 1.2 miles, a narrow side path — marked by a white-sand streak up through the trees — cuts left (west) up through a stand of hemlock to the summit of a high dune ridge. The 25-yard climb is a rigorous, sandy slog up the very steep back side of the ridge, with sand-buried cedar and balsam limbs poking up to provide handholds the final near-vertical yards.

The potentially breathtaking scramble is rewarded with breathtaking views down the throat of a narrow "blowout," one of several deep scars that have changed the once-straight crest of this mile-long dune ridge to zig-zag. The U-shaped indentations are formed when plants that stabilize a dune face are injured or destroyed, allowing the wind to blast the unsecured sand farther inland. Human footprints can initiate or exacerbate the process, and for that reason, signs throughout the area advise staying off the dune faces. Panoramic views from the crest of this 50-foot-high blowout sweep from midbay north and east through Harbor Springs to Wequetonsing (p. x).

From the crest, backslide down to the main trail and turn left (north). On the left 20 yards down the needle-covered path is a grand, old, 70-foot-tall hemlock followed on the right, 15 yards farther by an even-larger canted maple. From here it's a 300-yard walk straight north on the sidewalk-wide trail back to the boulder-bordered trailhead at the Dunes Campground and then another 300 yards down the east (rightmost) campground road and out the entrance gate back to the parking loop.

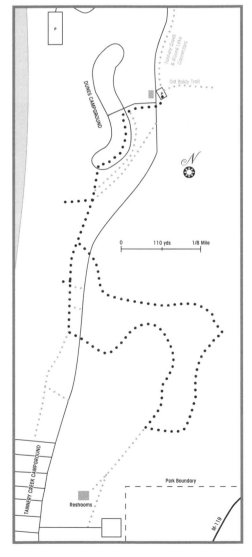

OLD BALDY

A rigorous rise to the summit of Petoskey State Park's highest dune, with literal tip-top looks. The peak views from the tip of the bay turn exceptional during fall color. And leafless seasons turn the perspective into a one-of-a-kind panorama.

LOOP TRAIL 0.5 MILES

ALLOW 30 MINUTES

Facilities: One rest bench at the overlook. Facilities elsewhere in the park include picnic areas, two modern campgrounds, and a beach area with bathhouse (including restrooms), a children's playground and concession area.

Directions: From the junction of M-119 and US-31 go north on M-119 1½ miles to the entrance to Petoskey State Park. Turn left (west) onto the entrance road and go 300 yards to the contact station (daily or annual vehicle permit required for entry). Continue straight another 300 yards to a fork. Turn sharply left (south) and go 250 yards to the camper registration building area. Just before reaching the building, bear left (east) into a parking area loop. The trail begins at the northeast side of the loop.

From the parking area the trail bridges a small gully, then immediately climbs nearly 50 wood stairs, platforms and bridges that connect a series of ridgetops, crossing over gullies and ravines in between. From the top of the stairs and platforms the trail follows the crest of a ridge on a wide, sandy, needle-covered path deeply shaded by hemlock, with help from the grape-leaf-size foliage of several Striped Maples. The trail rises gently, then moderately, then steeply about 150 yards to another set of 100 stairs and platforms that go straight up Old Baldy's sandy face — covered with a thick beard of pine, birch, hemlock, maple and Red Oak — to an overlook with a bench.

Sweeping but partially obstructed views take in the bay (p. *x*) from Petoskey to Harbor Springs. To the left (southwest), limbs and foliage frame the stark-white Inn at Bay Harbor, which from this perspective — 5 miles away and 170 feet above — appears to be perched on the shore like a Victorian-era cardboard cutout.

From the overlook, walking is a slip-sliding slog on soft sand 50 yards up to the summit, at 0.2 miles. There, a short path to the left (east) leads to a wide, sandy natural platform that in summer offers only glimpses through a thick stand of oak 160 feet down the dune's near-sheer backside onto M-119 and across to Round Lake (pgs. 56 and 73).

But during leafless seasons, the view from here, 770 feet above sea level, is like no other in the area, sweeping nearly unobstructed from the north end of Round Lake around some 235 degrees to Harbor Springs. And while standing at the top of this dune, you may also be standing on top of the remains of an Odawa Indian Chief who, according to legend, is buried here, also in a standing position facing the bay.

From the peak the sandy trail descends southwest 275 yards through oak and birch — with nice views of Petoskey and the bay through the trees — to skirt a small, round, sand-bottomed depression dotted with dune grass and a few shrubs and saplings. Though U.S. Geological Survey maps still label the area a "sewage lagoon," the dried-up area obviously has not been used as such for some time.

From there the soft, sometimes needle-covered trail enters the shade of hemlocks and twists and drops steeply — with exposed hemlock roots occasionally forming a few natural steps — 150 yards to the paved Tannery Creek Campground road. Twenty-five yards before the road, a well-worn trail branches off right (north) and winds through the woods 100 yards back to the parking area. Take either that path or the road.

(For more information on the formation of Old Baldy and other area dunes, see p. 64.)

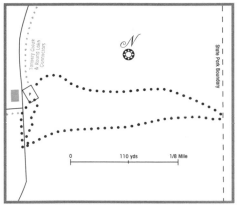

Dune Interpretive Walk

The Petoskey State Park sand dunes had a frigid birth. At the beginning of the end of the million-year-long Ice Age, the last of four worldwide glaciers advanced slowly south. On our continent they moved through Canada, scraping, stripping, gouging, and plucking millions of tons of boulders, pebbles, sand, clay, and other pieces of the earth along the way. And as the mile-thick ice sheets transported the debris over hundreds of miles and thousands of years, they also crushed, ground and mixed their cargo.

When the last of the glaciers melted and retreated from northern Michigan, beginning some 14,000 years ago, they dumped and spread the massive earthen mixture, laying the foundation for the region's current land features.

The receding, melting glaciers also created a series of pre-Great Lakes whose geologically frequent, sometimes dramatically varying water levels — both higher and lower than present — altered, sorted, and separated the deposits. For centuries, sometimes millennia, the lakes' powerful waves crashed their shores, scouring and pulverizing rocks. Silt settled to the deep lake bottoms, and massive amounts of sand washed up at the waters' edges.

About 5,000 years ago one of the last of the prehistoric lakes, named Nipissing, covered this area to a depth some 25 feet higher than present, its waters reaching a half mile farther inland. As the land here rebounded after being depressed into the earth's semi-molten core by the tremendous weight of the glaciers, Lake Nipissing correspondingly dropped in level. Exposed sand along the lakeshore dried, and prevailing winds that swept across the bay from the west moved it. Beginning about 4,800 years ago, the persistent winds pushed, rolled, bounced, and sometimes lifted specific-size (.01-.02 inches in diameter) grains of sand eastward. When the clean, fine, wind-blown particles hit nearby earthen debris remaining from even-more-ancient lakebeds, the sand piled on. It continued piling on for nearly 4,000 years, ultimately creating a row of seven parabolic-shaped sand mountains — with current heights of 700-770 feet above sea level — that line the east edge of the state park and extend north another half mile.

As the land here rebounded further, Lake Nipissing again dropped in level, exposing more sand and, beginning about a thousand years ago, a second set of dunes developed about ¼ mile west of the high, parabolic dunes. This time the wind-swept sand, having no earthen structures to pile onto, formed into a 30- to 50-foot-high ridge that parallels the tip of the bay.

Both sets of dunes — except the exposed west face of the foredunes — then became stabilized, as vegetation, beginning with grasses, evolved through plant succession to the present forests. Predominantly oak and maple now hold the parabolic dunes in place. And a palisade of cedars and pines along the crest of the foredunes plus hemlock, maple and oak that spill down their steep inland backsides has mitigated the otherwise relentless advance of windblown sand.

And finally, not much more than a century ago but more than 2,000 years after the Great Lakes had stabilized at their current level, another sugar-sand ridge formed, about halfway between the older foredunes and present-day shoreline. Those near-bare, 15- to 20-foot-high dune newborns are tenuously held in place by little more than dune grass.

The three rows of dunes here, with the others along hundreds of miles of Michigan's Great Lakes coastline, form the world's largest collection of freshwater coastal dunes.

LOOP TRAIL 1¼ MILES
ALLOW 1 HOUR

Facilities: A bathhouse (including restrooms), children's playground and concession area are located at the north edge of the south beach-area parking lot. Facilities elsewhere in the park include picnic areas and two modern campgrounds.

Directions: From the junction of M-119 and US-31 go north on M-119 1½ miles to the entrance to Petoskey State Park. Turn left (west) onto the entrance road and go 300 yards to the contact station (daily or annual vehicle permit required for entry). Continue straight another 300 yards to a fork. Again continue straight (west) and wind 0.2 miles to the beach parking areas. Bear left into the south parking lot.

The route begins at the south edge of the parking area between "no off road vehicles" and "no glass containers or animals" signs and travels about 0.6 miles south between the higher, older back (east) and lower, newer front (west) foredune ridges before returning north between the front dunes and the beach.

Even on a day that's too cool and windy for a walk on the lake side, the valley between the ridges can be comfortable. The front dunes block the wind, and heat generated by the sun-baked sand can elevate temperatures a good 10 degrees.

The protection from wind also makes this interdunal trough a bit more hospitable to plant life then elsewhere on the dunes. Still, conditions are brutally extreme. Summer sun can heat the sand to a scorching 100-plus degrees, also simultaneously drying out the ground. After sunset the sand rapidly releases the heat, making even midsummer nights potentially frigid. And being composed almost entirely of the mineral quartz, sand here offers no, and holds few nutrients. And any vegetation that does sprout risks being buried by drifting sand. Only the toughest, most-tenacious, most-specialized vegetation grows here.

By far the most-common and possibly the most-important plant here is the thick-, coarse-leaved Marram (dune) Grass. Marram takes root easily, propagates efficiently, grows quickly, spreads aggressively, stabilizes the sand, and creates a friendlier environment for other vegetation. And it's durable. A waxy cover protects the plant from sand blasting. And by growing up to 10 feet tall (here, waist-high

at its tallest) via a series of widely separated stem structures called nodes, the plant can be buried by shifting sand more than three feet per year and still survive.

The area is also rife with two stages of Tall Wormwood. During its first year, the biennial grows as lacey, ground-hugging, pale-green clumps. The following season, those that survive winter or sand burial produce 2- to 3-foot-high stems circled with fuzzy, needle-like growth plus short, upward-pointing branches that are bent over in late summer by hundreds of tiny, ragweed-like green and yellow flowers.

Many other kinds of wildflowers — some of which can only be found in dunes — also decorate this interdunal area, including Lesser Stitchwort, Pitcher's Thistle, and Spotted Knapweed.

Scattered shrubs along the interdunal section include circular clumps of flat-topped Ground Junipers, a few mats of low-growing Bearberry, willows, a couple of tangled patches of grape vines, and Sand

Cherries that, when covered with delicate white blossoms in early June, put on a beautiful show.

A clump of sand cherry, in fact, sprouts at the edge of the parking lot asphalt and again on the front dunes to the right of the signs. Just steps farther, a dozen-stemmed Lesser Stitchwort — whose tiny, cleft, white flowers top 18-inch reddish stems — pokes out of the sand on the left.

Just a few yards in, the face of the back dunes has been scarred by the first of many U-shaped indentations that vividly point out how fragile these huge sand piles are. Whenever plants that stabilize dunes are injured or destroyed — by fire, disease, drought, and other natural and human-caused accidents and incidents — the wind blasts the unsecured sand farther inland creating what is called a blowout. Human footprints can initiate or exacerbate the process, and for that reason, signs throughout the area advise, "help us stop erosion; stay off the bank." The dozens of blowouts along these back dunes have changed their once-straight crest line to zig-zag.

The blowouts have also exposed evidence that this row of dunes grew to its current height in stages, according to research recently conducted by Dr. Alan Arbogast of Michigan State University. The Assistant Professor of Geology's dating of thin layers of black, decayed organic matter that stripe the blowouts has revealed that about both 300 and 500 years ago, vegetation that had covered the ridge during periods of stability was buried during times of activity when wind-blown sand further built the dunes.

For the next 0.2 miles the route follows a walkway formed mostly by lag gravel, that is smooth stones and pebbles left behind after winds have removed most of the

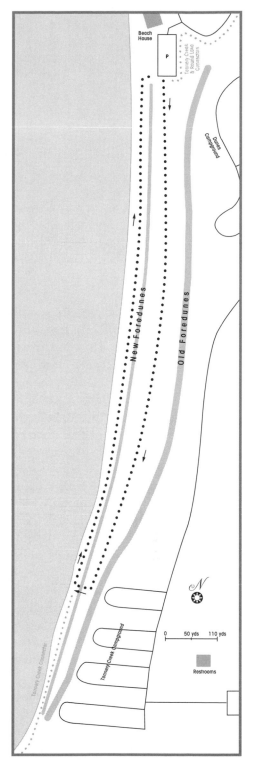

lighter, finer sand.

And it's easy to tell which way the wind blows here. The limbs of pines that top the back dunes sweep dramatically to the left (east) like windblown hair, lacquer-sprayed to permanence. At 200 yards the route passes the largest blowout — a 50-foot-wide, 75-foot-deep hollow crisscrossed by snow fences placed to halt or at least minimize further expansion. The effort is evidently working; tufts of dune grass have sprouted.

Growing at the crest of the lower front dunes directly opposite the large back-dune blowout is an isolated, exposed clump of 20-foot-high cedars that somehow have survived the brunt of the harshest elements. About 75 yards farther, a couple of large wind-toppled but still-living cedars lean against the back-dune bank near its base, their exposed roots sand-blasted to smooth, intricate natural sculptures.

Fifteen yards farther the gravel ends, and the route bears right, rising slightly toward a solitary, skinny young pine nearly devoid of limbs on the windward side. The remainder of the route is a tougher slog through sand (photo, above).

At 0.6 miles, cross over the front dunes on the first of three boardwalks that connect Tannery Creek Campground to the beach. The crest of the back-dune ridge has gradually fallen off until here it's at the height of the front-dune crest, about 15-20 feet above lake level.

At the boardwalk's end, turn right (north) and head back to the parking area. This stretch, too, is covered with lag gravel, washed ashore during recent former high-water periods, then blown clean during low water levels.

Far fewer plants grow along this harsher windward face. Sparser growth of Marram grass and Tall Wormwood here is interspersed with occasional wildflowers, willows, cherries, and a few isolated cottonwoods. And confidently poking out of the sand in the no-man's land between the gravel and moist beach are several Sea Rockets. The remarkable hardy annual — with almost-naked, yellow-green stems; thick, pod-like leaves; and tiny, delicate, lavender flowers — survives summer wind, waves, and human feet only to be washed away by winter storms.

And this stretch, too, is scarred by scores of blowouts, which often provide a cross-section look at the underworld workings of Marram Grass. The plant spreads by sending out fine, fibrous underground runners (called rhizomes) a few inches below and parallel to the surface. New shoots (called tillers) sprout up from the rhizomes every foot or so to form a snow-fence-type barrier that slows down blowing sand. When the sand piles up around and buries the plants, they send out another set of rhizomes and tillers. Over the years, the successive, intertwined, underground layers form a tight mesh that further helps hold sand in place. Near the top of the dunes along this stretch, wind and water have exposed large sections of Marram's fiber network, which looks like extensive nests of coarse steel wool.

STATE PARK BEACH COMB

A wide-open sandy, walk and/or a wet wade at the tip of the bay, with a perpetual panorama out over clear, Caribbean-colored blue-green water.

Facilities: A bathhouse (including restrooms), children's playground and concession area are located adjacent to the beach-area parking lot. Facilities elsewhere in the park include picnic areas and two modern campgrounds.

Directions: From the junction of M-119 and US-31 go north on M-119 1½ miles to the entrance to Petoskey State Park. Turn left (west) onto the entrance road and go 300 yards to the contact station (daily or annual vehicle permit required for entry). Continue straight another 300 yards to a fork. Again continue straight (west) and wind 0.2 miles to the beach parking areas.

This beautiful stretch of powder-sand shoreline — enjoyed by most in the warm summer sun — was brought here by a mammoth frozen earth mover.

At the beginning of the end of the Ice Age, glaciers on our continent moved slowly south through Canada, scraping, stripping, gouging, and plucking millions of tons of boulders, pebbles, sand, clay, and other pieces of the earth along the way. When the mile-thick ice sheets later melted and retreated some 12,000 years ago, they dumped the debris — in this area mostly as massive mounds called moraines, some with current heights of more than 1,200 feet above sea level.

The receding glaciers also created a series of pre-Great Lakes whose geologically frequent, sometimes dramatically varying water levels — both higher and lower than present   helped sort and separate the de posits. The lakes' powerful waves crashed the shores, relentlessly pounding the moraines and persistently breaking down quartz-bearing rocks into fine particles that were carried into the waters and combined to form sand. When the lake levels dropped, the sand was exposed to form beaches that, in turn, were exposed to the wind.

About 5,000 years ago one of the last of those pre-Great Lakes, named Nipissing, covered this area to a depth some 25 feet higher than present, its waves washing up on a sandy shore a half mile farther inland.

Prevailing westerly winds blew Nipissing's dry beach sand up and over earthen obstacles close behind, creating over the next 4,000 years, mountainous parabolic-shaped dunes. About 1,000 years ago, after Nipissing's level had dropped, exposing more sand, a second, 30- to 50-foot-high dune ridge developed about ¼ mile west.

And finally about a century ago, but more than 2,000 years after the Great Lakes had stabilized at their current-levels, the winds piled up another, smaller foredune ridge just yards from the water's edge.

Sometime during the last 2-3 millennia, American Indians also gradually moved into the greater bay area, eventually using it as a prime spring and summer hunting, fishing and farming grounds. In the early 1600s, Indians also began using the current state park land as a base to portage to Round Lake and then paddle birchbark canoes along a water trapping and trading route — then composed of Round Lake, a Round-to-Crooked-lakes stream, Crooked Lake, Crooked River, Burt Lake, Indian River, Mullet Lake, and Cheboygan River — to Lake Huron.

In 1855, shortly after the first white settlers began moving into the area, federal government treaties allowed local Indians to select lands, and the park area was deeded to a member of the Ottawa tribe named Pay-Me-Gwau.

About 20 years and a few changes of ownership later, the GR & I Railroad leased a strip of the land and, in 1882, completed a set of tracks that carried four trains a day from Petoskey to Harbor Springs across the beach only yards from the water.

Four years later, William W. Rice purchased the current park area and harvested the land's hemlocks for use at a leather tannery he opened at Tannery Creek, just west of the current park boundary. The tannery operated under various owners until 1950.

In 1934, during the Great Depression, tannery owners sold the water frontage here to the City of Petoskey, which opened a municipal park, the Petoskey Bathing Beach

However, the beach and bay waters were so badly fouled by the tannery's animal and other waste products that the company was later forced to build a discharge line to an inland settling basin, the remains of which can be seen along the Portage Trail (p. 59).

In 1962, 1¼ miles of shoreline and 305 inland acres were purchased by the State of Michigan, which removed the long-unused railroad tracks and developed the area into the current state park.

Almost all of the developed portions of the park are separated from the beach by the pair of foredune ridges. And so from a large change house, the park's wide band of nearly pure sand — which continues out far from shore under the water — stretches uninterrupted for a mile south and ¼ mile north. Crowds congregate in the beach-house area but thin quickly both ways along the water, except for occasional beach-chair and -blanket colonies at the south end where three boardwalks connect to the Tannery Creek Campground.

Waves pushed by prevailing westerly winds wash up an assortment of flotsam and jetsam here, including shells, occasional sand- and water-polished stones, remains of marine life, driftwood, and refuse from summer boat traffic. And from the campground section of beach south to the park boundary and beyond (see p. 54, Tannery Creek connector), fall storms and spring ice-out also deposit large numbers of rocks both on the shore and in the water. The collection includes Petoskey Stones, which quickly get picked over and out.

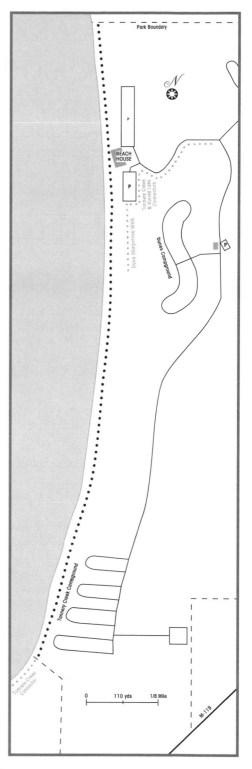

ROUND LAKE NATURE AREA TO PETOSKEY STATE PARK

A short route that links the Round Lake Nature Preserve trails (p. 73) to Petoskey State Park's trails (pgs. 59-69) plus the Tannery Creek Connector (p. 54).

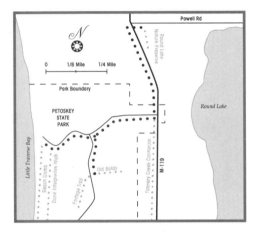

DISTANCE TO TANNERY CREEK CONNECTOR 0.5 MILES

DISTANCE TO OLD BALDY AND PORTAGE TRAILHEADS 1 MILE

DISTANCE TO BEACH COMB AND DUNE INTERPRETIVE TRAILHEADS 1.1 MILES

Facilities in the state park include picnic areas, two modern campgrounds, and a beach area with bathhouse (including restrooms), a children's playground and concession area.

Directions: From the junction of US-31 and M-119, go north on M-119 1.8 miles to Powell Road. Turn right (east) onto Powell and go ½ block to the entrance road to the Little Traverse Conservancy offices, on the right (south). Parking is available near that log-sided building.

From the parking area, head north about 75 yards back out the entrance road to Powell Road. Turn left (west) and follow along Powell about 50 yards to M-119. Carefully cross the busy highway to the Little Traverse Wheelway, an asphalt pathway that currently runs 12 miles from Bay Shore to just 175 yards north of here at Beach Road. Plans call for the route to ultimately link Charlevoix to Harbor Springs.

Turn left (south) onto the Wheelway and follow it ⅓ mile to the state park entrance road and the junction with the Tannery Creek Connector. Turn right (west) onto the entrance road, which passes a contact station in 300 yards, then gently winds and drops another 300 yards to a fork. To get to the Old Baldy and Portage trailheads, bear left and follow the road about 250 yards to the camper registration building area. To reach the Beach Comb and Dune Interpretive Walk, continue straight about 0.2 miles, twisting and dropping between some 10- to 30-foot-high sand dunes, to the beach parking area.

ROUND LAKE NATURE PRESERVE

A trio of trails combined into a single near-level route through a range and variety of plant communities, including a high, dry mixed-hardwoods/conifer forest; a wetter lowland cedar swamp; and water-soaked bog.

Added pluses are sweeping views across Round Lake and labeled identification of a dozen of the Petoskey area's most-common trees.

LOOP TRAILS 1¼ MILES
ALLOW 1 HOUR

Facilities: None

Directions: From the junction of US-31 and M-119, go north on M-119 1.8 miles to Powell Road. Turn right (east) onto Powell and go ½ block to the entrance road to the Little Traverse Conservancy offices, on the right (south). The trailhead is just south of that log-sided building.

For further details about this Little Traverse Conservancy preserve, pick up a brochure at the trailhead and return (recycle) it when done. Since 1972 the non-profit conservancy has purchased and preserved the natural beauty of 12,000 acres of diverse Northern Michigan land.

A platoon of Red Oaks stands guard at both sides of the trailhead, scattering acorns around the base of the entrance sign. From there the wide, soft trail enters the 60-acre preserve in the shade of a mixture of hemlock, Balsam Fir, and a few birch, Largetooth Aspen, beech and Red Oak. For the next 0.7 miles the route parallels M-119, 150-200 yards from the busy highway.

At 100 yards the trail forks; continue straight (south). Two hundred twenty-five yards farther, just after the trail turns sharply left (east), the trail again forks. Bear sharply right (south) through a more-open area of predominantly pine, aspen, maple, and a few balsam and beech.

At ¼ mile the route reaches the base of a looped section. Bear right (southwest) onto a narrow, shadier trail through an area littered with fallen trees. On the right (west) at 0.4 miles is a good-size, labeled Black Cherry, characterized by its unique "burnt potato chip" bark.

Seventy yards farther the path breaks out into a small, open area blanketed by waist-high ferns and nearly surrounded by 30- to 40-foot-tall white pines. (A well-worn trail south from here leads 40 yards to private

property.) In spring the meadow is home base for squadrons of flitting dragonflies. And in summer, legions of mosquitoes bivouac throughout the nature area.

From the fern field the trail turns sharply, looping (north) almost back upon itself, passing first through a small stand of 40-foot-tall pines then briefly through maples and aspen. For the next 250 yards the path moves past a mixture of predominantly beech, maple, and white pine on the left. On the right for most of the same stretch, a 20-yard-wide band of the same trees plus hemlock separates the trail from a lowland filled with 10- to 20-foot-tall saplings. White pines in this section include some 2½-foot-diameter, 75-foot-tall behemoths.

At 0.6 miles the trail forks. Continue straight (north) 125 yards, past several skinny Striped Maples on the left (west), to another fork. Turn sharply right (east) onto the south leg of a large-looped trail that drops through a damp, dense and cool stand of hemlock to another fork, at ¾ mile.

Bear right (east) to Round Lake on a trail that winds and drops between lowland hardwoods, on the right, and another sapling-studded lowland, on the left. The path then briefly follows the top of a small ridge that drops on both sides to lowlands quilled with young trees.

At ⅜ mile the route reaches a boardwalk that winds and sometimes bounces 100 yards, first between the lowland saplings, then over an even-wetter area, and finally across a bog, to an observation platform at the shore of Round Lake. Panoramic views across the shallow, blue-green, sand-bottomed waters sweep from high moraines to the south to wooded, near-lake-level flats to the east and north. The vista occasionally includes a pair of swimming loons that nest here.

A small, shallow pond behind (west of) the platform is a classic example of how all contained water bodies ultimately become solid land by filling with runoff sediment and with vegetation that grows, dies, falls to the bottom and produces peat. The depression ultimately becomes so full of the mucky matter that surface water no longer stands in it. Cattails, rushes, and other aquatic plants grow first, fronted quickly by Water Lilies, Duckweed, and other floating plants. When the peat they create becomes solid enough around the pond edges, water-loving shrubs, then trees take over, which forces the aquatic plants farther out into the water. When the outer rings have encroached to the point that there's no longer enough water to support the aquatic plants, the water body has officially become a swamp, which eventually will become dry land.

This once-large pond — which is connected to the lake during high-water periods — has filled in over the centuries to reduce its size to only 30 feet in diameter. Reeds and cattails ring the edges, lily pads cover a quarter of the remaining water surface, and reddish-brown muck forms a tenuous bottom and some shoreline.

From the observation platform, backtrack to the large-looped trail and bear right (north), following the north leg of the loop. Sixty yards farther, the trail touches the towering corpse of an 18-inch-

diameter tree whose barkless, sun-bleached, white skeleton has been perforated by woodpeckers boring for a bug buffet. A few of the holes that are large and rectangular were routed by Pileated Woodpeckers, the distinctively noisy, crow-size species that inspired the cartoon character Woody Woodpecker.

Ten yards farther, touching the trail on the right, is a Yellow Birch that is characteristically growing out of a rotting, moss-covered "nurse" stump. When the host stump completely decays, the birch (and a companion younger balsam) will perch on their exposed roots.

From there the trail twists — sometimes almost back upon itself — along available high ground through a cedar/hemlock swamp, with boardwalks across potentially wet areas, then gradually rises to a higher, dryer, more-open area of beech, maple, aspen and oak before reaching a junction at 1.2 miles. Turn right (north) and return 100 yards to the trailhead.

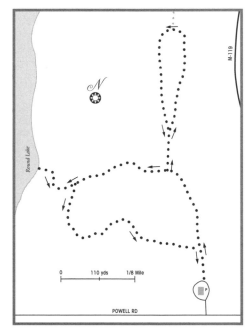

MAGNUS CITY PARK TO BAYFRONT PARK

A varied route that includes the opportunity for Petoskey-stone hunting, a close-up look at the area's oldest building, a one-of-a-kind look at the city from the tip of a breakwater, views into the mouth of the Bear River, and a water-craft inspection — all backdropped by near-continuous, panoramic perspectives of the bay (p. x)

ROUND TRIP 3.2 MILES, INCLUDING TO THE TIP OF THE BREAKWATER; 2.7 MILES WITHOUT

ALLOW 2 HOURS, INCLUDING TO THE TIP OF THE BREAKWATER; 1½ HOURS WITHOUT

Facilities: Restrooms and water are available at Magnus and Bayfront parks. Restrooms are also available at the back (north) side of the police/fire department building, on the west bank of the Bear River at the pedestrian bridge. A concession stand at the south end of the Bayfront promenade is open during softball games.

Directions: From the junction of US-31 and US-131, drive north then east on north US-31 0.7 miles to a traffic signal at Lake Street (the second signal after crossing the Mitchell Street Bridge and curving left, north). Or from the junction of M-119 and US-31, drive west on south US-31 2.6 miles to the traffic light at Lake, (the next light after passing a softball field, on the right). Turn west onto Lake and follow it 0.9 miles to the west end of Magnus City Park.

Drop over the edge of the parking area a few yards to the rocky bay shore, one of the area's most consistently good spots to search for Petoskey stones. The official state rock is actually petrified coral that lived in a warm salt-water sea that covered Michigan 350 million years ago. The fossil's characteristic gray-green, white-bordered, hexagonal markings can best be seen when wet, so successful hunters dodge waves at the water's edge, wade out into shallow areas, and even search shores in the rain. Spring ice-out and major fall storms wash in fresh specimens, which range from thumbnail- to boulder-size.

At the east end of the 300-yard-long

beach, head up right (south) to the park's entrance contact station, then turn left (east) onto a sidewalk along the north side of Lake Street. The route passes Northern Michigan Hospital, up to the right (south), then on the left (north), a half dozen contemporary waterfront homes, the last of which is one of the most-palatial residences to be found within the city. Just two lots farther, also on the left, a picket fence encloses the city's oldest building, the St. Francis Solanus Indian Mission, built in 1859 (further details, p. 108).

A hundred twenty-five yards farther, Lake Street intersects Ingalls Avenue. Turn left (north) onto Ingalls and go about 50 yards to where it dead-ends at Water Street. Turn right (east) onto Water, which edges a grassy field on the left (north) then curves gently around the Fraternal Order of Eagles clubhouse, on the right. The street then passes briefly between a small, old manufacturing building, on the right, and Sunset Shores condominiums and a relic railroad

building, on the left, to Wachtel Avenue. Turn left (north) onto Wachtel and go about 150 yards to the foot of Petoskey harbor's protective breakwater.

It is permissible to walk to the end of the nearly quarter-mile-long structure when its surface is dry. It is potentially dangerous to do so when the walkway is wet from precipitation or wave splashes or especially when high winds send water crashing over the top of the structure.

The first 100 yards of the breakwater consists of a 15- to 20-foot-wide pile of hundreds of huge, near-rectangular chunks of limestone (possibly from a quarry that once operated not far down the shore) mixed with a few granite boulders and topped by a concrete sidewalk. The final 300-plus yards is constructed of 33 conjoined 25-foot concrete sections, each with a flat 4- to 5-foot-wide center "sidewalk" that angles down three feet from each edge to narrower walkways whose barrierless edges drop abruptly three to five feet —

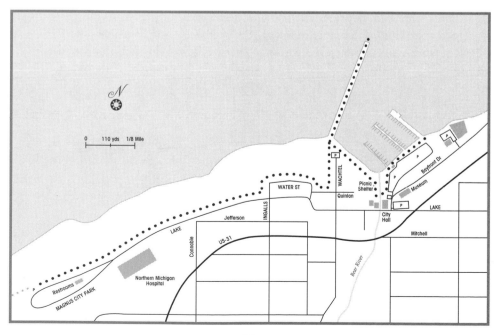

depending on lake level — to the water. Narrow, but deep grooves between each of the sections plus the fact that their tops don't align perfectly make for potential trips.

Twenty-five feet from the breakwater's end, a plain, white, 4-foot-diameter, metal cylindrical light tower rises 25 feet from a 7-foot-high, red, rectangular concrete base.

On shore from the foot of the breakwater, the route drops to the left (east) of a small parking area and heads southeast — near the water's edge on a sandy (during low water) stretch of beach or a large, open grassy area behind — 150 yards to a picnic pavilion overlooking the mouth of the Bear River.

This is not the place nature chose for the Bear to join the bay. For more than two millennia until 1892, the Bear swept into the big water some 150 yards east. The rivermouth was then relocated to here, and the Chicago and Western Railroad filled in the old channel and a portion of the bay to create the site for their Victorian-style depot, now a museum (see p. 107).

From the pavilion, the route follows a sidewalk south up to and then east across a pedestrian bridge over the river to behind city hall. On display in a glass case at the back of the lobby of that building (entry a block south, off Lake Street) is a beachball-size Petoskey stone.

From the pedestrian bridge the route follows the sidewalk east 50 yards to a diversion wall, built out into the water in 1991 to prevent river sediment from filling in the harbor. The sidewalk continues along a rip-rap retaining wall that edges the municipal marina shoreline, where a pair of piers poke 175 yards out into the water. It is permissible to walk out onto the diversion wall or piers for closer looks at craft — from small fishing boats to lots of sailboats to 50-foot yachts — that seasonally or daily tie up at 100 slips.

The turnaround point for this route is the marina launch area, near Bayfront Park's main promenade, which runs south from under a 62-foot-high tower holding 8-foot-diameter clock faces and a 500-pound bronze bell that have shown and rung the time of day since 1902, first above the (now demolished) City Hall/Emmet County Courthouse building, then the Little Traverse History Museum, and now here.

RESORT TOWNSHIP EAST PARK TO MAGNUS CITY PARK

A walk on a former railroad bed atop a high bluff, with elevated, water's-edge, often-panoramic perspectives of the bay. Parks at each end of the route are a double bonus.

ROUND TRIP 2.8 MILES

ALLOW 1½ HOURS

Facilities: Restrooms and water at both ends, in season.

Directions: From the junction of US-131 and US-31, drive west on south US-31 1.4 miles to the entrance road to Resort Township East Park, on the right (north). Turn right (north) onto the entrance road and wind 275 yards to a road that leads right (east) to a parking area and restroom building.

From the restroom building, on the southeast side of the parking area, head south 15 yards on a woodchip-covered path, then turn left (east) onto a gravel path that connects 15 yards farther with a perfectly straight asphalt trail. (An asphalt path that branches off left here connects with the Gazebo Bluff Trail, p. 84). The main route continues straight (east) through a tunnel of young birch, ash, elm, and a few maple about 200 yards to a bridge across a 3-foot-wide creek that spills out of a cedar thicket on the right (south) and drops four feet in a series of miniwaterfalls over rock ledges.

From the asphalt's end 15 yards farther, the route continues straight (east) on a wide dirt and gravel path about 100 yards to the township park's eastern boundary.

Though the abandoned railroad bed from here is commonly viewed and used as a public right of way, sections totaling 1,900 feet over the next mile are private property whose owners could prevent the public from trespassing. The owners have not yet done that, and so it is important to respect the private property — especially by staying on the main trail — so that the route remains accessible.

From the park boundary the trail continues another 35 yards to the Arrowhead Shores private residential development's small asphalt cul de sac, at ¼ mile. The route crosses the drive and 125 yards farther breaks into the open onto a 0.2-mile-long stretch of sustained sweeping views down the throat of the bay (p. *x*) from the edge of a bluff that drops nearly vertically 40 feet to the rocky shore.

To the right (south) the banks rise steeply, also sometimes nearly vertically, as much as 50 feet up to US-31, though the busy highway is rarely seen or heard.

At just past a half mile, views of the bay are abruptly reduced to glimpses through a thick growth of mostly young cedar. And from here the trail gradually drops to near water level at Magnus Park.

At 0.7 miles, where the trail drops and rises gently and quickly through a sandy washout, the bay again comes into open view. A hundred twenty-five yards farther, birches, aspen, a variety of low-growing shrubs, and later, cedar and pine hide the water until just before reaching Magnus City Park.

At ⅞ mile the trail passes by and over a large wood, concrete and metal flume that drains the area from above. And just past a mile the path crosses in front of condominiums on the bluff high above. Side trails down to the water, here, are private.

About 150 yards before reaching the west end of Magnus City Park, the route again breaks into the open. Conspicuous in views to the west from here is the imposing Inn at Bay Harbor (p. 90), which appears to be perched on the shore like a Victorian-era cardboard cutout.

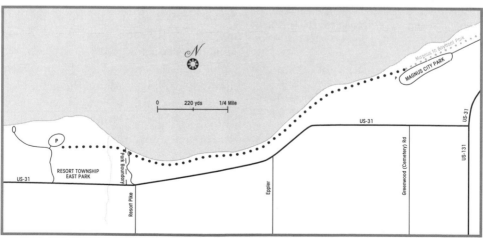

COASTAL CREEK TRAIL

A short, but varied stroll through a tunnel of trees, past a small waterfall, along a clear creek, and across a bay bluff.

ROUND TRIP ½ MILE

ALLOW 30 MINUTES

Facilities: Restrooms, picnic tables and pavilion, water, and one rest bench, at the waterfall. Plans call for the addition of 40 more parking spaces, a second picnic pavilion, a children's playscape, and more trailside benches.

Directions: From the junction of US-131 and US-31, drive west on south US-31 1.4 miles to the entrance road to Resort Township East Park, on the right (north). Turn right (north) onto the entrance road and wind 275 yards to a road that leads right (east) to a parking area, pavilion, and restroom building.

From the restroom building, on the southeast side of the parking area, head south 15 yards on a woodchip-covered path, then turn left (east) onto a gravel path that connects 15 yards farther with a perfectly straight asphalt trail. (An asphalt path that branches off left here connects with the Gazebo Bluff Trail, p. 84).

The main route continues straight (east) through a tunnel of young birch, ash, elm, and a few maple about 200 yards to a bridge across a 3-foot-wide creek that spills out of a cedar thicket on the right (south) and drops four feet in a series of miniwaterfalls over rock ledges.

Fifteen yards farther east, where the asphalt ends, bear sharply left (north) onto a woodchip-covered path, which forks just a few feet farther. Take the left (west) path, which angles about 20 feet through ash, maple and cedar to the edge of the creek, where the trail then turns right (north). A berm blocks sight and sound of the flow for the next 15 yards until the trail breaks out into a meadow, where a scraggly, old apple tree hunches under the protective limbs of a tall, lone ash, on the right. Now visible to the left, the fast-flowing creek drops through a 10-foot-deep, sandy-banked minicanyon.

From here the path gently rises past a clump of 10-foot-tall sumacs, on the right, then descends a few yards through a colony of 50-foot-tall Trembling (Quaking) Aspens, whose leaves even in the slightest

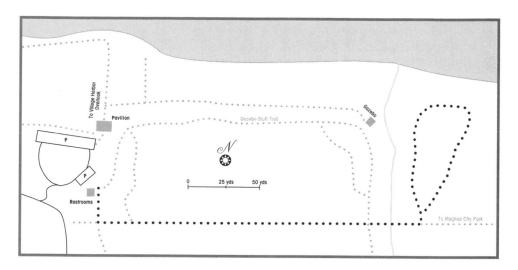

breeze make a sound like soft rain falling on a metal roof. For the next 125 yards, small, potentially toe-stubbing stumps regularly poke out of the settling woodchips that cover the newly constructed trail.

From the aspens, the trail drops steeply through cedars to a sharp bend right (east), directly across the creek from an observation gazebo (p. 84). The path continues through a thicket of young cedars as it traverses a bluff about 40 feet above the bay, with glimpses of the water coming through gaps in the growth.

At just past ¼ mile the trail turns 90 degrees right (south) and rises moderately to steeply as it winds through a heavy growth of mature cedars about 60 yards to another old apple tree, on the right (west), opposite its partner across the small meadow.

From here, the route moves about 30 yards through a stand of ash and maple to a fork. Continue straight (south) a few feet to the blacktopped former railroad bed, turn right (west) and follow it back to the restroom building.

GAZEBO BLUFF TRAIL

A short route — half of it paved — that packs in close contacts with the bay, a coastal brook, and a magnificent maple forest.

LOOP TRAIL 0.4 MILES
ALLOW 30 MINUTES

Facilities: Restrooms, picnic tables and pavilion, and water. The asphalt sections of this trail are specifically designed to accommodate wheelchairs. As such, the use of all other wheeled devices — such as bikes, in-line skates, and scooters — are prohibited along the paved sections, except the railroad bed. Plans call for the addition of 40 more parking spaces, a second picnic pavilion, a children's playscape, and trailside benches.

Directions: From the junction of US-131 and US-31, drive west on south US-31 1.4 miles to the entrance road to Resort Township East Park, on the right (north). Turn right (north) onto the entrance road and wind 275 yards to a road that leads right (east) to a parking area, pavilion, and restroom building.

From the restroom building, on the southeast side of the parking area, take the asphalt path that heads east, then immediately curves gently left (north) toward the bay. In just the next 100 yards, as the path skirts a picnic pavilion then curves to follow the edge of a bluff 40 feet above the water, it passes through a natural mini-arboretum that includes American Elm, Northern White Cedar, Sugar Maple, Trembling (Quaking) and Largetooth Aspen, White Birch, ash, and Hop-hornbeam, whose unusual bark looks like it's been put through a paper shredder and then glued in vertical strips onto the trunk. The thick growth allows only glimpses of the bay through this section.

At 50 yards a short, paved trail to the right (south) connects to the park's main east-west trail, a blacktopped former railroad bed. At 175 yards, just before the junction with another connector trail, a magnificent White Ash towers over the path, on the right.

Thirty-five yards farther a branch trail descends left a few feet to a gazebo, tucked into a small cedar grove overlooking a small but fast-flowing brook that drops through a 10-foot-deep, sandy-banked minicanyon. The picturesque panorama also includes good looks north across the bay (p. *x*) and west to the Inn at Bay Harbor (p. 90), but views to the east, including the brook's merger with the big water, are blocked by a thick growth of cherry, willow and cedar.

From the overlook the route heads south and follows the creek bank through basswood, maple, and ash. At the trail's left edge about 25 yards from the gazebo is a clump of birch with the distinct, dark-gray remains of inch-diameter unidentifiable saplings tightly coiled around some of the trees' white-barked trunks and limbs. Directly across and 15 feet off the trail to the right is another such skinny sapling, which spent years snaking around and up an aspen only to die and leave a rope-looking corpse that still chokes its moribund host.

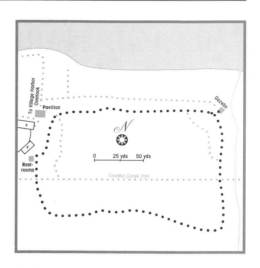

At 0.2 miles the path intersects the straight-as-an-arrow former railroad bed then rises steeply but briefly on a wood-chip-covered path that plunges into a stand of majestic Sugar Maple. The straight, limbless trunks of the stately sentinels stretch up 50 feet to crowns that canopy and deeply shade the forest floor.

About 50 yards after leaving the asphalt, the path twists sharply right (west), then serpentines 225 yards through the maples and, over the last 50 yards, Hop-horn-beam.

Edging the trail on the right about halfway through the woods, as the grassy banks up to the park's entrance road come into full view, is a maple with a large, abnormal growth called a burl, about 10 feet up the trunk. Likely the result of a long-ago injury, the large, wartlike scar has developed a distinctive, swirled grain pattern highly prized for creating bowls, artwork and veneer. Many other maples throughout the woods here are also burled.

Village Harbor Overlook

A short, open walk over terraced bluffs, with panoramic views of Lake Michigan, Little Traverse Bay, and the east end of Michigan's newest ultra-luxury resort development.

LOOP TRAIL ½ MILE

ALLOW 30 MINUTES

Facilities: Restrooms, picnic tables and pavilion, and water, plus benches at the small-boat launch area. Plans call for the addition of 40 more parking spaces, a second picnic pavilion, a children's playscape, and more trailside benches.

Directions: From the junction of US-131 and US-31, drive west on south US-31 1.4 miles to the entrance road to Resort Township East Park, on the right (north). Turn right (north) onto the entrance road and wind 275 yards to a road that leads right (east) to a parking area, pavilion, and restroom building.

From the parking loop, four open, grassy plateaus terrace down about 40 feet to the bay shore. From the northeast corner of the parking area (the fourth and top plateau), head for the picnic pavilion (on the next, third, shelf) and take the steps that drop about four feet to it. Move through the pavilion and continue straight (north) to 16 steps that drop about ten feet to the second terrace. A trail that heads right (east) from here leads to the base of an observation gazebo (p. 84). Continue straight (north) about 15 feet to the the final set of steps, which drop about 25 feet to a gravel path across a wide, mowed-grass plateau next to and only feet above the bay.

Turn left (west) onto the gravel path and go about 200 yards to a small parking lot at the park's boat-launch area, at 0.2 miles. The route continues straight (west) across the asphalt, then rises gently to another wide, mowed path that continues west along the base of a 15-foot-high grassy bluff.

About 150 yards from the boat launch area, the route reaches a fork. Continue straight (west) a few feet to a fence about 15 feet from the edge of and about 15 feet above a 50-yard-long channel that connects Lake Michigan to Village Harbor, which marks the east boundary of Bay Harbor, a seven-year-old, billion-dollar luxury resort and residential development. (For more details about the Bay Harbor area, see pgs. 86-97.)

Backtrack to the fork and turn right (south). The route rises and narrows as it follows the park boundary fence south about 35 yards, then bends sharply left (east). Centering the elevated views west from here is the sock-shaped, sheltered harbor, created from a long-abandoned quarry.

Wrapping the west end and on around between the harbor and the Great Lake on the north is Lakeshore Village, one of 29 named Bay Harbor neighborhoods.

Farther west is the imposing, stark-white Inn at Bay Harbor, a condominium hotel whose more than 130 suites — with fireplaces, kitchens and balconies — can be individually purchased (cost: $300,000-$1,100,000) and then rented to temporary hotel guests when not used by owners.

To the south, a bluff rises vertically, as high as 40 feet, just yards from the harbor shore. Perched at the edge of the layered-limestone cliff, deposited some 350 million years ago when Michigan was covered by warm saltwater seas, is a half-mile-long row of half-million-dollar-plus Victorian condominiums.

From the overlook the trail leads east about 60 yards to a T junction with a gravel path. Take the path left (northeast), rising about 35 yards to where the trail twists sharply back right (southeast). Views of the bay from this high point are sweeping (p. x).

From the overlook the path gradually descends southeast about 100 yards then jogs sharply left (east) and drops steeply a few yards to the asphalt boat-launch entrance road. The route continues straight (east) across the road then connects to a path that rises about 40 yards to a T junction. Turn right (south) onto a gravel path that rises about 20 yards then turns left (east) and leads 60 yards to a set of steps up to the west end of the parking area or another 60 yards to the picnic pavilion.

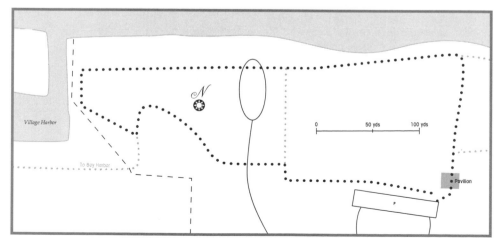

BAY HARBOR

> *Close encounters with the public parts of an otherwise private, gated ultra-luxury resort and residential development created out of industrial dust.*

LOOP TRAIL 2½ MILES

ALLOW 1½ HOURS, NOT COUNTING SHOPPING STOPS

Facilities: Food facilities in Bay Harbor's (downtown) Marina District include gourmet takeout, a cafe/coffee shop, a pub, and an upscale restaurant.

Directions: From the junction of US-131 and US-31, go west on south US-31 2.2 miles to the entrance to the Bay Harbor ("shopping, dining, lodging") Marina District, on the right. Follow the entrance road, Bay Harbor Drive, ¼ mile down to just a few yards before passing between the green post office building, on the right and the Original Pancake House, on the left. Turn left (west) there into a parking lot behind a large, brown building decorated with large flag-patterned awnings. If that lot is full, park across Bay Harbor Drive behind (east of) the post office.

Head west through the parking area behind (south of) the large, brown building to the blue-gray Harbormaster Building, recognized by its distinctive stone peak capped by what look like inverted clay pots. A nautical-theme gift shop and a casual restaurant, Knot Just a Bar, fill most of the glass-enclosed ground floor, and a sinuous glass-railed deck wraps a quartet of $1½-million second-level condominiums.

Circle counterclockwise around to the water side of the Harbormaster Building, then walk to the end of the leftmost (southmost) of two piers that stretch more than 250 yards out into Bay Harbor Lake, created in 1995 by spectacularly blasting a short, 160-foot-wide channel to allow water from Lake Michigan to fill an old quarry. A hundred twenty-five slips spaced along the pair of piers comprise a transient, reservations-accepted public marina that can accommodate vessels up to 150 feet in length. The state-of-the-art "floating" docks can also be hydraulically height-adjusted to match the lake's varying levels.

A hundred yards from the south shore, layered-limestone cliffs, deposited some 350 million years ago when Michigan was covered by warm saltwater seas, rise 40 feet to support a 300-yard-long row of million-dollar-plus Victorian condominiums.

At the southwest corner of the 90-acre, 80-foot-deep, sheltered harbor, the Bay Harbor Yacht Club is fronted by 128 private slips divided among five piers. Those "dockominiums" are purchased (price: $200,000-500,000), not rented, by boaters who use them as home port and sometimes home. Those who choose to live on their craft, live well. The long list of amenities there includes hook-ups for cable TV, internet, telephone, electric and water, plus use of the Yacht Club's spa, tennis courts, swimming pool, fitness center, restaurant, and other facilities.

Sprawling west for nearly three miles from the harbor's sunset end are a trio of 9-hole, world-class golf courses, wrapped by 18 of Bay Harbor's 29 distinct, named neighborhoods. In view from here due west are the 4th green and 5th fairway of The Links course, atop a high bluff.

Palatial mansions that surround Bay Harbor Lake contribute substantially to the 1,200-acre development's estimated $1 billion worth. A half dozen of the most-striking estates perch on a thin strip of limestone that separates the Great Lake from the harbor. Many dwellings here are the second, sometimes third homes of an

international list of owners. And most of these getaways have not been built with old, seasoned money or by "trust fund babies." Most Bay Harbor property owners are relatively young 35- to 55-year-old nouveau riche.

Return to shore, taking note along the pier of how dockhands form ropes into textbook examples of sailors' knots and coils. On land, angle left (northeast) of the Harbormaster Building 150 yards across a grassy park to Main Street, which runs between a pair of uniquely designed, block-long, four- to five-story-high combination shopping/dining/residential structures that make up Bay Harbor's Marina District. For a decade until 1994 this site was an awful sight — a huge, rusting, crumbling, abandoned, century-old cement plant surrounded by mountains of kiln dust and acres of bare limestone pitted with quarries.

Head east up cobbled Main Street on either the bright, white (north) side or the shadowy, layered-chocolate-with-white-icing south side. Filling the lower levels on

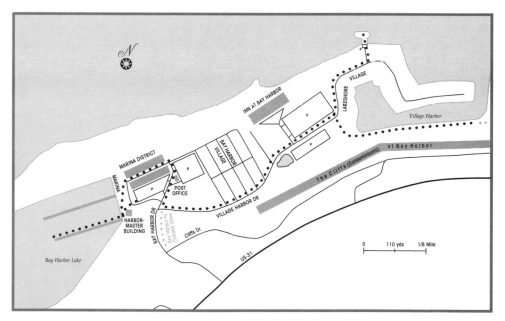

both sides are restaurants, a gourmet market, galleries, and more than a dozen and a half upscale shops offering nautical collectibles, books, clothing, footwear, furnishings, fine jewelry, china, antiques, designer eyeware, and other specialty merchandise.

Round, copper-trimmed Juliet balconies — illuminated by double-masted, nautical-like blue lights — protrude from upper levels on the white side. Rectangular balconies up on the brown side are recessed. All exit from some 75 furnished luxury suites — ranging from one-bedroom units to a 7,000-square-foot, eight-bedroom penthouse — that can be rented or purchased.

At the east end of Main Street, turn right (south) and follow Bay Harbor drive 125 yards to the junction with Village Harbor Drive. Turn left (east) and follow Village Harbor Drive, which gently winds between Bay Harbor Village, a 61-lot neighborhood on the left (north), and a layered-limestone cliff rising 30-40 feet on the right (south). Strung along the edge of the clifftop is a half-mile row of $500,000-plus Victorian condominiums.

A quarter mile from Bay Harbor Drive, Village Harbor Drive passes a small quarry pond on the right. To the left several hundred yards across a large parking lot is the imposing, stark-white Inn at Bay Harbor (photo, right), which is a condominium hotel. That is, each of the Victorian facility's more than 130 luxury suites — with fireplaces, kitchens and balconies — can be individually purchased (cost: $300,000-$1,100,000) and then rented to temporary hotel guests when not in use by the owners.

Two hundred yards farther, at one mile, the road reaches an archway entrance to Lakeshore Village, a small neighborhood designed to replicate the closely spaced look and close-knit feel of a Nantucket-like seaside community. All 36 lots are waterfront — 20 on the bay and 16 wrapped around the toe of sock-shaped, sheltered Village Harbor, another former quarry. The harbor sites also include private boat docks and ready access to the bay through a short channel.

Follow the village road, which curves 150 yards north then 125 yards east, to a public observation/fishing pier, on the left (north). Turn left (north) and walk 100 yards out to the concrete pier's end, with sweeping views of the bay area (p. x).

Backtrack to Village Harbor's archway entrance, at 1.4 miles, then take a footpath that heads 100 yards southeast — between a home, on the left, and a small grassy bluff, on the right — to the southwest corner of the harbor. The trail then drops to a concrete sidewalk that runs 100 yards between 11 boat slips, on the left, and the fossil-filled limestone cliff, on the right. From the sidewalk's end, a quarry-gravel path continues 275 yards east across a narrow strip of land between the cliff and the water to the turnaround point, at the harbor's east edge, at 1.7 miles. Occasionally visible through breaks in cedars that line the trail on the right (south) is water that "weeps" out of the limestone to wet the rock below and color it with green velvet moss.

BAY HARBOR TO COASTAL DRIVE

> *A gently winding, all-asphalt route past a mix of wealth, business, industry, and scenery.*

ROUND TRIP 3.4 MILES

ALLOW 2 HOURS

Facilities: Abutting the path ¼ mile west of the entrance road is a service station with restrooms, a convenience store, and deli. Food facilities in Bay Harbor's (downtown) Marina District include gourmet takeout, a cafe/coffee shop, a pub, and an upscale restaurant.

Directions: From the junction of US-131 and US-31, go west on south US-31 2.2 miles to the entrance to the Bay Harbor ("shopping, dining, lodging") Marina District, on the right. Follow the entrance road ¼ mile down to the green post office building, on the right, and the Original Pancake House, on the left. Turn right (east), just before the post office, into a large public parking lot.

From the parking area, walk on the asphalt sidewalk up, alongside the east side of steep, winding Bay Harbor Drive (the entrance road). To the left (east), layered-limestone cliffs, deposited some 350 million years ago when Michigan was covered by warm saltwater seas, rise 50 feet to support a row of half-million-dollar-plus condominiums.

Good views, also to the east, of the imposing, stark-white Inn at Bay Harbor come from the intersection with Cliffs Drive, about halfway up Bay Harbor Drive. The luxurious Victorian facility is a condominium hotel. That is, each of its more than 130 suites — with fireplaces, kitchens and balconies — can be individually purchased (cost: $300,000-$1,100,000) and then rented to temporary hotel guests when not in use by the owners.

At ¼ mile, just a few feet before reaching pillars that mark the Bay Harbor Marina District entrance, the sidewalk reaches the Little Traverse Wheelway, an asphalt path that closely parallels US-31 on the highway's north side. Views north across the bay (p. *x*) are good from here. Dominating the shore directly below is the brown backside of one of a pair of uniquely designed, block-long, five-story-high combination shopping/dining/residential structures that make up downtown Bay Harbor. Until 1994 that Marina District

was the sight of an abandoned century-old limestone quarry and cement plant. (For additional details about the Bay Harbor area, see pgs. 86-97.)

Head right (west) on the Wheelway, across Bay Harbor Drive, then past the Northview Design Center, on the right (north) about 225 yards farther. Upscale specialty tenants at that retail/office complex include builders, architects, designers, and retailers of top-of-the-line home-design products such as flooring, faucets, fixtures, appliances, custom cabinetry and millwork, and home theatres.

Fronting the contemporary strip of suites at the west end is a quaint throwback gift shop that sells dried fruit products and a selection of classic up-north souvenirs, with emphasis on rocks, stones, and agates plus jewelry and other items made out of those natural materials.

At ½ mile the path crosses over the entrance road to Manthei Veneer Splicing Division, whose 150 employees manufacture single-ply hardwood veneers shipped to furniture, window, and other manufacturers such as Broyhill and Andersen. The trail then plunges into a 50-yard-long natural corridor formed predominantly by 30- to 40-foot-tall Jack Pines, then passes the gravel back-entrance road to the large Manthei complex, which also includes a Redi-Mix (concrete) Division.

Seventy-five yards farther, the path edges a dense grove of cedar, on the right (north), studded with a few large maple, ash, aspen, White Birch, and a couple of Gray Birch.

At ¾ mile the cedar forest ends where the path crosses the entrance to one of Bay Harbor's 29 gated, private, named neighborhoods, Harborview Ridge.

Thirty-five yards farther, just off the trail to the right are the home offices of the John R. Watson Development Company, the largest builder in Bay Harbor. The firm has constructed condominiums at The Cliffs, Harborview Ridge, and Quarry View developments as well as many spectacular individual homes throughout the 1,200-acre, billion-dollar resort and residential development.

From there the path drops and rises quickly, crosses a gravel service road across

US-31 from Lake Grove Road and, at 0.9 miles, reaches the entrance to Petoskey Plastics Inc., on the right. Inside the sprawling complex, more than 100 employees manufacture thin, strong engineered-plastic products such as reclosable "zipper" bags, retail merchandise bags, trash compactor bags, and the huge recycle-collection bags used by grocery stores and others to return beverage containers to distributors by the thousands. The 30-year-old firm also operates its own in-house recycling center, which transforms old plastic bags into usable raw materials.

At one mile the route crosses the back entrance to the firm and, less than 100 yards farther, gently winds past a Bay Harbor tennis court complex, with glimpses through the chain link fence at some of the palatial seasonal homes that perch on a thin strip of limestone separating the bay from manmade Bay Harbor Lake. At 1.2 miles, where the path sharply curves about 15 yards before reaching the entrance gate

to the Bay Harbor Yacht Club, is the only place you can look down at the short channel that was spectacularly blasted in 1995 to allow water from Lake Michigan to fill an old quarry and create the 90-acre, 80-foot-deep lake. Nice views of some of the fabulous homes around its shore come from the entrance gate area.

At 1⅓ miles the path reaches a 100-yard long, curving, wood fence, on the right (north), that separates the trail from Bay Harbor's Wild Winds Drive, just a few feet away. About halfway along the fence, the bay and the 5th fairway of The Links golf course come into nice but brief view.

From the end of the fence for the next ¼ mile the path rises gently as it passes by the modest (by Bay Harbor standards) $285,000-$325,000 homes in the Wildwoods subdivision, then reaches the turnaround point — a 50-foot-long, 7-foot-high, 10-foot-wide corrugated-metal culvert that carries vehicle traffic over the trail on Coastal Drive to the Bay Harbor golf clubhouse.

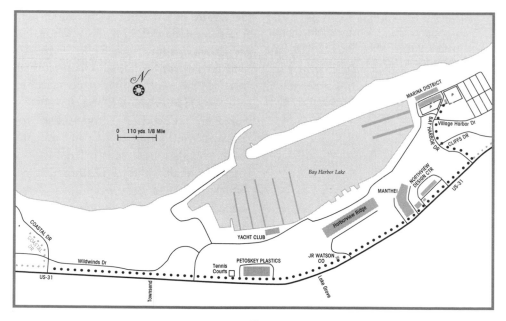

93

Coastal Drive

> *Unique perspectives of the bay come from this open, winding walk through sections of a luxury resort community created out of industrial dust.*

ROUND TRIP 1.6 MILES

ALLOW 1 HOUR

Facilities: Public facilities at the otherwise-private clubhouse include restrooms at Arthurs 27, a casual pub and grill with views over The Quarry course's 9th-hole green and sand trap to the bay.

Directions: From the junction of US-131 and US-31 go west on south US-31 approximately 3.7 miles to the Bay Harbor Golf Club entrance road, on the right (north). Turn right (north) onto the entrance road and go a block to a gatehouse, which during warm-weather months is staffed with security personnel who will allow you to enter. Follow Coastal Drive approximately 0.9 miles to the Golf Clubhouse parking area.

From the parking lot, head back northeast along Coastal Drive, which is level for the first couple of hundred yards, then drops briefly and steeply toward the lakeshore. On the left (northwest) at 300 yards are summer homes and available lots that help make up The Pines, one of 29 named neighborhoods in the 1,200-acre Bay Harbor luxury resort and residential development, which stretches along five miles of Lake Michigan shoreline. A few yards farther, Coastal Drive passes Pines Court, the private entrance road to The Pines million-dollar lakeshore lots.

Continue on Coastal Drive, dropping gently toward the lake, then bearing right (east) to follow a 0.2-mile-long wood barrier that snakes along the water's edge across the road from a 30- to 50-foot-high grassy bluff. Spread across the blufftop, but not in view from the roadway, are the 1st and 7th fairways of The Links, one of three diverse 9-hole golf courses that combine to rank Bay Harbor as one of the country's — some say the world's — top golf experiences. In view a mile and a half across the water straight ahead (east) is Bay Harbor's downtown, the Marina District (p. 88), which until 1994 was the sight of an abandoned, century-old limestone quarry and cement plant. Behind and to the left (north) is the imposing, stark-white Inn at Bay Harbor condominium hotel (p. 90).

At ⅓ mile, just beyond the east end of the wood barrier, a temporarily lone, pala-

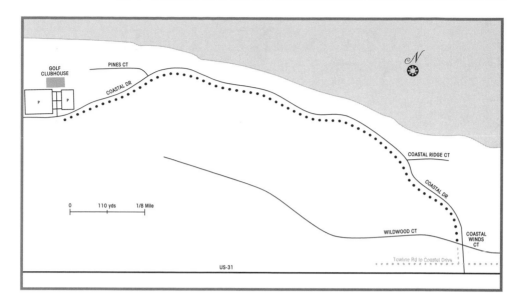

tial summer residence is the westmost of ten lakeshore lots (priced from $650,000) that help make up the Coastal Ridge community. From here the road briefly and gently rises and drops, then gradually curves right (southeast) and rises steadily for the remainder of the route. At 0.6 miles, Coastal Ridge Court, a private entrance into Coastal Ridge, branches off to the left (east).

Ninety yards farther, an asphalt golf cart path tunnels under the roadway. (On the return route, cross over here from the shoulderless left [west] side of busy, narrow, winding Coastal Drive to the wider grassy median on the right [east] and walk on that side until reaching the west end of the wood-fence barrier, just before Pines Court.)

One hundred twenty-five yards farther, at ¾ mile, the route turns south where, to the left (east), the 6th-hole fairway of The Links points the way to distant high hills.

A hundred yards farther, Coastal Drive reaches the turnaround point at Coastal Wood Court, which goes right (west), and

Wildwinds Court, which goes left (east). Just a few yards beyond (south of) a nearby gatehouse, Coastal Drive crosses over a huge corrugated-metal culvert that carries Little Traverse Wheelway walkers (pgs. 91 and 96), bikers, and other nonmotorized traffic under the road.

TOWNLINE ROAD
TO COASTAL DRIVE

A long, near-level walk on an open asphalt strip that separates the area's busiest highway from the state's newest ultra-luxury resort development.

ROUND TRIP 5 MILES

ALLOW 2½ HOURS

Facilities: Several rest benches are spaced along the route. A convenience store is located south across US-31 from the parking area. Restrooms and water are available at Resort Township West Park, 1,000 feet north on Townline Rd.

Directions: From the junction of US-131 and US-31 drive west on south US-31 approximately 6.2 miles to Townline Rd., at Bay Shore. Turn right (north) onto Townline and immediately turn left (west) onto an informal, dirt parking area.

From the parking area, cross Townline Road to the current west terminus of the Little Traverse Wheelway, an asphalt pathway that runs east without interruption 12 miles to just north of Petoskey State Park. Plans call for the route to ultimately link Charlevoix to Harbor Springs.

Seventy-five yards in, the straight trail passes the first of many rest benches spaced along the route. For most of the remainder of the route, the trail is also lined with aspens, including large numbers of the Trembling (Quaking) variety. Even in a slight breeze, their fine-toothed leaves' gentle rustle — like the sound of rushing water — can nearly drown out the sounds from the highway. To further buffer traffic noise, pines and spruces have been planted, on the right here, but on both sides along the entire route.

Also, on the left (south) for the next ¾ mile — but unseen because of a 200-yard-wide, heavily wooded buffer strip — is the Preserve of Bay Harbor, the largest of the $1-billion luxury resort development's 29 gated and private neighborhoods. More than 50 building sites here overlook the nine-hole Preserve golf course, and another more than 30 nestle in mature hardwoods along the Lake Michigan shore. Lot prices range from a quarter of a million to more than a million dollars.

At a half mile the path begins a series of

gentle curves, and at one mile the route passes the entrance to the The Preserve community.

At 1.2 miles the trail veers right (south) to within a few yards of the highway, with only a grassy median between. To the left (north) are the cupola-topped Quarry Bluffs custom townhomes — 4,000-square-foot residences priced from a million and a quarter dollars. Glimpses of the bay come from between the structures and, for the next 300 yards, over the tops of manmade berms. Two hundred seventy-five yards past the east end of the townhouse row, a 10-yard-long gravel road connects left (north) through a break in the berm to asphalt Quarry Ridge Drive.

Another berm on the south side of that road blocks views of what may be the state's — and among the country's — most-unique and challenging golf holes. As its name indicates, the nine-hole Quarry course is constructed in, on, between, and around several former limestone quarries, cliffs and ponds. Shots from the 4th tee (which front-centers the townhouses), for instance, drop 50 feet over the face of a bluff onto a fairway shared with the 5th hole, whose first stroke must arc over a large pond and whose pitch to the green

must be launched to the top of the bluff.

At 1¾ miles, glimpses of the Quarry's first two holes come through aspens and a few birch. And 275 yards farther, across US-31 from Camp Daggett Road, a narrow, gravel service road heads about 25 yards to the tip of the golf club's practice range.

Across the highway a half mile farther, manicured lawns sweep up to Bay Harbor's horse "barn," a 42,000-square-foot stable and arena that is the centerpiece of the development's equestrian complex. The striking green-trimmed and -roofed building is sided with natural cedar shingles and stained cedar boards and is topped by windowed cupolas and shingled dormers. Surrounding the imposing hilltop structure are an outdoor track and acres of trails, all enclosed by miles of green-painted oak fences.

At 2½ miles, 200 yards after dropping slightly between earthen berms on each side, the route reaches the turnaround point, a 50-foot-long, 7-foot-high, 10-foot-wide corrugated-metal culvert that carries vehicle traffic over the Wheelway on Coastal Drive to the Bay Harbor golf clubhouse.

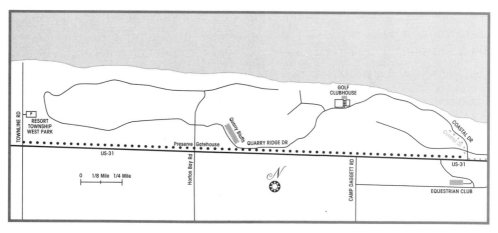

RESORT TOWNSHIP WEST PARK

A short, shady loop through a mature hardwood forest followed by a drop over a clover-filled meadow to a rocky, little-used, scenic section of bay shore.

LOOP TRAIL 0.9 MILES

ALLOW 1 HOUR

Facilities: Restrooms at the trailhead; picnic tables and pavilion at the shore. Plans call for the addition of benches near the shoreline and a boardwalk trail over the wetland.

Directions: From the junction of US-131 and US-31 drive west on south US-31 approximately 6.2 miles to Townline Rd., at Bay Shore. Turn right (north) onto Townline and go 1,000 feet (0.2 miles) to the Resort Township Park West entrance road, on the right (east).

Just a few yards from the parking area's east end, take the wide, woodchip-covered path to the right (south), which rises and falls, sometimes steeply, as it serpentines ¼ mile through a heavily shaded hardwood forest. Sugar Maple and Trembling (Quaking) Aspen (including some formidable specimens) predominate, but there are also good numbers of White Birch and hemlock, plus a few beech and an occasional Yellow Birch, identifiable by its yellowish-gray, horizontally peeling, curling bark. Seedlings of this species can establish themselves in rotting logs, stumps, and even moss on rocks. A 14-inch-diameter specimen at the trail's edge on the left 25 yards from the trailhead, for instance, grows out of a decomposing stump whose remnants are still obvious. On the right 35 yards farther, a smaller tree, also at the trails edge, sprouted out of a now almost completely rotted, moss-covered log.

At 175 yards, about 10 feet after the trail turns sharply left and begins a steep drop, a Striped Maple leans against a bare aspen trunk about six feet off the trail to the left. At 1½ inches in diameter and 15 feet tall, the maple specimen — characterized by large, three-lobed leaves and smooth, greenish-white, vertically striped bark — is larger than most. A favorite deer food, the understory shrub doesn't commonly survive to grow much past the mostly 2- to 4-footers spaced along the rest of trail. (Striped Maples are particularly easy to spot in fall when their hand-size leaves turn to a distinctive creamy-yellow color.)

Fifty yards farther, the trail rises steeply to the top of a ridge, where a section of the 5th-hole fairway of Bay Harbor's The Preserve golf course is visible through the tree trunks to the right. A hundred seventy-five yards farther the path turns sharply left (west), drops steeply again, and passes between a pair of 8-foot-tall, ½-inch-diameter Striped Maples at the junction with a gravel trailroad, at ¼ mile.

Turn right (north) onto the trailroad which, 50 yards farther, turns into a two-track that drops across a wide, open meadow toward the bay shore. Fifty yards farther, a mowed path branches off right (northeast) 50 yards to a few stairs that drop to an overlook at the edge of a former quarry, now a wetland nearly filled with cedars. A second (closer to the bay) mowed path heads from the overlook straight (west) back to the two-track, which continues descending along the precipitous edge of the old quarry toward a picnic pavilion.

Fifty yards before reaching the pavilion, another mowed path heads off 60 yards right (east), passing through a small stand of young Trembling (Quaking) Aspen before reaching a 100-foot-long, 20-foot-wide, shallow, marshy pond, usually filled with frogs and ducks.

Backtrack from the wetland along the path to the two-track, then continue north another 75 yards to the park's 600 feet of rocky Lake Michigan shore that offers good Petoskey Stone hunting. Views (see p. *x*) from here are excellent west to Nine Mile Point, north to the Harbor Springs

area, and east to the white-sand beaches of Petoskey State Park.

The return to the trailhead is a 0.3-mile-long, 75-foot rise on the two-track, then a gravel road through maple, aspen and birch.

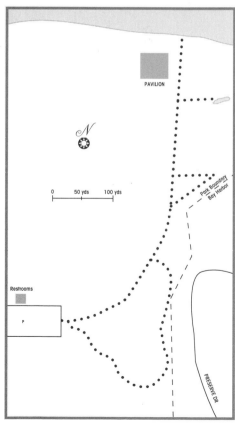

CURTIS FIELD

The Petoskey High School (Curtis Field) track is the perfect place for walkers to take a measured try at life in the fast lane. At exactly ¼ mile around the inside of the dead-level oval, it's easy to accurately determine your walking speed, stride or distance.

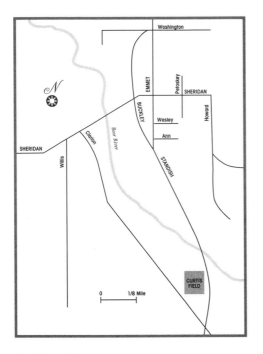

Simply measure the time in minutes and seconds and count the number of steps that it takes you to walk one lap. Calculate your stride by dividing 1,320 feet by the number of steps. If you took 528 steps to complete one lap, for instance, your stride is 2.5 feet. To figure your per-mile walking pace, multiply the time by 4. If it took you 4 minutes to walk one lap, you walked at a brisk 16-minute-per-mile clip. And of course to walk any exact distance, multiply the distance by 4; that's how many laps you will have to walk. Three miles, for instance, requires 12 laps around the asphalt.

The track is open to the public 8:30 a.m. to 8 p.m., Monday-Friday, during school summer vacation months.

Facilities: None

Directions: From the junction of US-31 and US-131, go south on US-131 0.5 miles to Sheridan. Turn left (east) onto Sheridan and go 0.4 miles to Buckley (just after crossing the bridge over the Bear River and then railroad tracks). Turn right (south) onto Buckley and go ⅛ mile to the junction of Emmet and Standish. Bear right (southeast) onto Standish and go 0.4 miles to the football field/track complex, on the right (west), 2 blocks after crossing the river.

GASLIGHT GALLERY WALK

An enlightening stroll through nine distinctly unique Gaslight-area galleries and studios plus a visit to the hub, headquarters, and heart of the area's cultural community. An added plus: during one evening each June, you can also sip wine and graze on gourmet goodies while making the rounds.

LOOP ROUTE: 1 MILE

ALLOW 2-3 HOURS

Facilities: Public restrooms are located behind the Chamber of Commerce building, on the northeast corner of Mitchell and Howard. Plenty of food and beverages are available throughout the Gaslight District.

Directions: From the junction of US-31 and US-131, drive north then east on north US-31 0.7 miles to a traffic signal at Lake Street (the second signal after crossing the Mitchell Street Bridge and curving left, north). Or from the junction of M-119 and US-31, drive west on south US-31 2.6 miles to the traffic light at Lake, (the next light after passing a softball field, on the right). Turn east onto Lake and go three blocks to a metered parking area on the left (north), at the east edge of Pennsylvania Park and across the street from the City Park Grill.

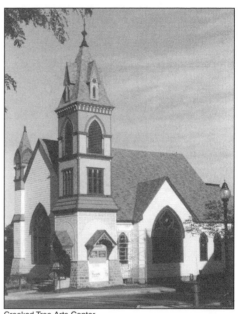

Crooked Tree Arts Center

From the parking area, walk west on Lake about a half block to Park Avenue, a cement sidewalk on the west side of Pennsylvania Park. Turn right (north) and head about ½ block to the **Gardiner, Rackham & Steele** gallery/studio at 218 Park. Using mixed mediums but predominantly watercolors, owner/artist Doug Flewelling paints traditional scenes of British Isle and local landscapes as well as historic brick and stone local buildings. Flewelling also features works by other Michigan artists.

Exiting Gardiner, Rackham & Steele,

101

turn left (north) and go about ½ block to Bay Street. Turn left (west) onto Bay and go one block to Howard Street. Cross (west) Howard to the **Perry Sherwood Gallery** (200 Howard St.), at the southwest corner of Bay and Howard. A continually changing inventory of contemporary art and home and office accessories as well as fine art is elegantly showcased in their large, open display space. Unique works include fountains, mobiles, sculptural glass, ceramics, jewelry, original paintings, and limited-edition prints. A small, open upstairs balcony holds smaller pieces and sale items.

From Perry Sherwood, backtrack east across Howard, turn right (south), and walk ½ block to the **Artery** (207-A Howard). Specialties here are steel sculptures and an outstanding collection of art glass. Works by more than 50 artists also include original oil paintings, limited-edition lithographs, and wall sculptures.

From the Artery, turn left (south) and go just a few yards to the **Whistling Moose** (209 Howard). A wide range and tremendous variety of nature-inspired art and handcrafts takes two stores worth of space to hold. Works from more than 200 artists include original drawings and paintings, prints, photographs, books, carvings, bronzes, knives, gourds, pens, candles, tiles, and stationery. In the in-store studio, co-owner Hanni Yothers creates most of the 500 pieces of jewelry on display, plus decorative and functional handbuilt pottery with a signature pine design. Husband and co-owner John builds custom wood products, from small boxes to custom furniture to stunning mahogany water craft (photo, above), which sometimes hang from the ceiling.

From the Whistling Moose, turn left

(south) and walk to the corner of Lake and Howard. Turn right (west), cross Howard, and go ½ block on Lake to **Ward & Eis** (315 E. Lake). The aroma of fine leather permeates this corridor-shaped gallery. Contemporary and traditional works by nearly 200 top leather and other craftspeople from 36 states include designer handbags, briefcases, portfolios, wallets, organizers, and jewelry. Art from eight American Indian tribes includes Hopi sculpture, Zuni jewelry, Lakota wall hangings, and other unique wood, clay and stone creations.

From Ward & Eis, turn right and head west on Lake to Petoskey Street. Cross Petoskey to **Luciano Studio-Photographic Art,** on the northwest corner of Lake and Petoskey (221 E. Lake). Inside are custom-sized photographic prints of Italian landscapes, vistas, street scenes, and closeups of architectural features, all taken by the owner, native Venezian Luciano R. Duse.

Next door to Luciano on Lake is **Valerie** (219 E. Lake), which features Northern Michigan scenes and landscapes — which usually include signature, sometimes-subtle, sometimes-dominant florals — by impressionist oil painter Valerie Thompson.

From Valerie return (east) to the corner of Lake and Petoskey. Cross (south) Lake, turn left (east), cross Petoskey, and go one block east on Lake to Howard. Turn right (south) onto Howard and walk a few yards to **Northern Art** (306 Howard). Inside are a tremendous variety and sizes of prints, almost all with a northern Michigan feel — boats, flowers, wildflowers, woods, and water — though rarely of readily identifiable places. Northern Art also advertises that they carry the most extensive selection of creative framing in the north, including exquisite European frames gilded in gold.

From Northern Art, turn right (south) and go almost a block to the corner of Howard and Mitchell. Turn left (east), cross Howard, turn right (south), cross Mitchell, and walk ½ block south on Howard to the **Shadetree Studio** (417 Howard). Here, husband-wife team Penny Kristo and John Bowes create distinctive custom- and classically designed stained glass windows, doors, domes, lamps, skylights, privacy screens, and other pieces for homes, churches, and businesses. The gallery also carries smaller stained-glass gift items plus a selection of original oil, watercolor, and acrylic paintings plus tiles, including Pewabic.

From the Shadetree, turn right (north) and return to Mitchell. Cross Mitchell, turn right (east) and walk two blocks to the **Crooked Tree Arts Center** (461 E. Mitchell), at the northwest corner of Mitchell and Division. Inside the restored three-story, Victorian-style Methodist church, two galleries feature changing visual-art exhibits — some world class — on loan from other institutions and by Michigan artists, including locals. Centerpiece is a magnificent, intricately detailed basswood sculpture of an Odawa trapper. The Art Tree sales gallery offers a continually changing, eclectic mix of juried works by northern Michigan artists and Center members. The 15,000-square-foot Center is also home to an art school, six music studios, a pottery studio, and a 275-seat theater that hosts dance, music, and drama productions. (For more details on the Center, see p. 112.)

Late each June the Center is also the start and finish of a formally informal version of this walk, complete with street musicians along the route and gourmet hors d'ouvres and fine wines served at the gal-

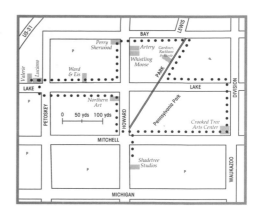

leries. Pick up a self-guided walking tour map at the Center and have it stickered at each gallery you visit. Back at the Center, each sticker gets you a raffle ticket and a chance at winning one of several fine-art pieces donated and awarded by the galleries at an Afterglow gathering. The Afterglow (as well as foreplay) at the Center also includes refreshments and musical and dance performances. For the date and time of the official Gallery Walk, contact either the Chamber of Commerce (347-4150), the Crooked Tree Arts Center (347-4337), or ask at any of the galleries.

To return to the parking lot from Crooked Tree, walk one block north on Division Street to Lake, turn left (west) onto Lake and go one block.

Gaslight Gift Shop Browse

An all-occasion treasure hunt through greater Gaslight-area shops guaranteed to have distinctly unique gifts.

Facilities: Public restrooms are located behind the Chamber of Commerce building, on the northeast corner of Mitchell and Howard. Plenty of food and beverages are available throughout the Gaslight District.

Directions: From the junction of US-31 and US-131, drive north then east on north US-31 0.7 miles to a traffic signal at Lake Street (the second signal after crossing the Mitchell Street Bridge and curving left, north). Or from the junction of M-119 and US-31, drive west on south US-31 2.6 miles to the traffic light at Lake, (the next light after passing a softball field, on the right). Turn east onto Lake and go three blocks to a metered parking area on the left (north), at the east edge of Pennsylvania Park and across the street from the City Park Grill.

Downtown Petoskey stores have continuously catered to resorters and other visitors for more than a hundred years. At the turn of the century, souvenir vendors and grocers lined streets that were illuminated by gasoline-fueled lamps. The area was called the Midway, and most shoppers arrived during the summer months by steamship or train. Today, northern Michigan's most-quaint, historical shopping destination is known as the Gaslight District, and tourists and vacationers drive here year round.

Nearly 100 shops and stores are concentrated in roughly 10 square blocks of well-preserved, turn-of-the-century Victorian brick buildings (p. 107), and replica gaslights now line most of the the streets. Proprietors are individuals, not corporations; some stores have been in the same families for generations; and owners are often also the clerks.

A wide range of retailers offer a tremendous variety of merchandise including clothing and shoes, toys and games, antiques, art (p. 101), jewelry, furniture, and specialty foods, to list just a few. And as independent general-interest booksellers approach extinction just about everywhere else, this small area supports two.

Following are brief descriptions of only those gift shops, boutiques, and specialty stores that consistently offer a continuous-ly changing selection of unique, often one-of-a-kind items. Most of these shops are also unique to Petoskey; that is, you won't find them or their merchandise anywhere else.

1. AMERICAN SPOON FOODS. An ever-expanding selection of what some say are the *world's* finest fruit products includes dried fruits, toppings, butters, relishes, sauces, salsas, jellies, jams, and preserves. American Spoon has earned earned national reputation and international recognition by developing and perfecting a field-to-table process that captures, concentrates, and preserves the natural flavor of select, superb Northern Michigan-grown fruits.

2. PARKSIDE NORTH. Small gift items, with emphasis on ceramics, including tiles, lighthouse replicas, and lots of winter-village pieces.

3. SYMONS GENERAL STORE. Gourmet, specialty, exotic, and hard-to-find foods from around the world — most bottled, canned, boxed, or otherwise packaged. A fine-wine shop fills a lower level, and a small deli features a selection of unique imported cheese, including a variety made from water-buffalo milk.

4. TOAD HALL. Two floors of small gift items and collectors' pieces, with emphasis on kitchen glassware such as goblets, mugs, plates, bowls, and platters. The varied inventory also includes a large selection of handpainted china and cut-glass.

5. BACK TO NATURE. Nature-themed decorative and functional items include lots of birdhouses and dried floral wreaths and other arrangements.

6. BASKET SHOP. Reed, cane, wicker, sea grass, and other natural materials woven into hundreds of different-sized and -shaped baskets, containers, furniture, furnishings, and other home accent and decorator items.

7. CUTLERS. Home-decor accent and practical items include handpainted china; top-of-the-line gourmet-kitchen cookware; silver and stainless trays, platters, bowls, and other serviceware; cut glass and Waterford Crystal; and a variety of photo frames. A large selection of other items includes jewelry and wedding-theme and baby gifts.

8. J.W. SHORTER MERCANTILE. A select sampling of Grandpa Shorters' wares, plus packaged turn-of-the-century-type food items.

9. GRANDPA SHORTERS. An eclectic array of gift and practical items with an up-north, outdoorsy look and feel are loosely arranged by themes, such as hunting, fishing, lighthouse, nautical, and kitchen. A large selection of polished Petoskey-stone items ranges well beyond jewelry, and the back fourth of the main level is filled with a wide assortment of moccasins. The lower-level Trappers Cabin stocks furniture, furnishings, gifts, and decorative accessories with a cottage or cabin look.

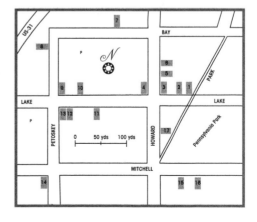

10. CAPRICORN MOON. Beads, books, jewelry, small sculpture, fragrant oils and oil diffusers, incense and incense burners, and other New Age items.

11. PICKETT FENCE. A continuously changing, eclectic selection of unique, often one-of-a-kind, small home furnishings, indoor and outdoor accent pieces, and decorator items.

12. COUNTRY CLUTTER. A wide range and variety of small home-made and home-made-looking items are grouped by themes such as nautical, garden, bears, kitchen, and bath. Shelves are also stocked with dolls and miniatures, candles and holders, home-accent pieces, and in-season holiday decorations.

13. IN THE WOODS. Carvings, sculptures, decoys, toys and games, birdhouses, and other home-accent, gift and utilitarian items, almost all made of wood.

14. SHOW OF HANDS. A wide range of homemade and homemade-looking arts and crafts items includes in-season holiday decorations, home-accent pieces, lots of rubber stamps, kitchen accessories, pottery, quilts, and baskets.

15. BEN FRANKLIN CRAFTS. A tremendous number, variety, and range of craft materials for children through adults includes paper die cuts, miniature doll houses and furnishings, yarn, ribbon, fabric and trims, cross-stitch supplies, frames, colored and patterned glass, dried and artificial flowers, an assortment of basket- and straw-hat-weaving materials, and brushes, paper, paint, and other artists' supplies.

16. ETHNIC CREATIONS/JEDEDIAH'S ANTIQUES & COLLECTIBLES. Two formerly stand-alone stores combined space in year 2000 to sell their wares separately together. Their large, long, open retail space is informally split down the middle on two levels. Ethnic Creations' half is stocked with natural-fiber clothing, musical instruments, jewelry, sculpture and carvings, candles and holders, incense and burners, mirrors, and other home-accent furnishings and decorator pieces — predominantly Indonesian in origin, with some African and North and South American items.

Jedediah's half is neatly crammed with a wide assortment of small and large antiques.

17. SHALIMAR IMPORTS. An eclectic, wide-ranging, and varied selection of small gift items from around the world includes sculpture, wood carvings, masks, perfume bottles, mobiles, jewelry, and clothing.

AROUND
THE BUILDING BLOCKS

A walking tour past, and sometimes optionally inside, Petoskey's most-historical and architecturally unique or significant structures, most of which have been beautifully and accurately restored and/or maintained.

LOOP TRAIL 2¼ MILES

ALLOW 2 HOURS

Facilities: Public restrooms are located behind the Chamber of Commerce building, on the northeast corner of Mitchell and Howard. Plenty of food and beverages are available throughout the Gaslight District.

Restrooms and water are also available at the Bayfront Park building, just east of and across Bayfront Drive from the pedestrian tunnel exit.

Directions: From the junction of US-31 and US-131, drive north then east on north US-31 0.7 miles to a traffic signal at Lake Street (the second signal after crossing the Mitchell Street Bridge and curving left, north). Or from the junction of M-119 and US-31, drive west on south US-31 2.6 miles to the traffic light at Lake, (the next light after passing a softball field, on the right).

Turn west onto Lake and go one block to Bay Front Drive, on the right, just before city hall and the river. Turn right (north) onto Bay Front and then immediately turn right (east) again onto Depot Court, which leads into a parking area behind the Little Traverse History Museum.

The building that houses the Little Traverse History Museum (1) was constructed as a depot for the Chicago and West Michigan Railway in 1892, during the peak years of train travel to Petoskey. Its shingle-sided, two-story entry tower is topped by a conical roof, is fronted by a covered area for passengers dropped off by carriage, and is flanked by gray, glazed-brick, single-story waiting areas. A wood veranda wraps the structure.

Exhibits inside include a collection of small, Ottawa-made birchbark boxes beautifully decorated with dyed porcupine quills; a mural that depicts the local, turn-of-the-century seasonal slaughter of passenger pigeons, which contributed to the bird's extinction; and permanent and changing displays built around the theme, "People Who changed Emmet County."

Ernest Hemingway materials include photos, autographed books, and from

Windemere — a Hemingway family cottage on Walloon Lake where the author spent his first 18 summers — a child's writing desk, an old reading light, and a typewriter.

From the museum, walk west across the parking area to Bayfront Drive, turn left, and cross Lake Street to Mineral Well Park. A cream-and-rust-colored Victorian-looking pavilion (2) there is a remnant of what once was a thriving health-spa complex, where turn-of-the-century tourists came to treat kidney trouble, indigestion, and other ailments by soaking in and drinking sulfurous mineral waters.

About 100 yards south, the Mitchell Street Bridge (3) carries US-31 traffic over the Bear River. Built in 1930, the historic structure is the fourth-longest concrete girder bridge in the state, with two dozen massive columns supporting seven spans that total 330 feet in length.

From Mineral Well Park follow Lake Street west through Petoskey's oldest residential area ¼ mile to Ingalls Avenue. A half block farther west on Lake, a picket fence on the right (north) encloses the city's oldest building, the St. Francis Solanus (Catholic) Indian Mission (4), built in 1859. Twenty years later, a wood church was built ½ mile southeast across the river, but Ottawa Indians continued worshipping here until 1896. In 1931 the fieldstone foundation, clapboard siding, brick chimney, wood-beam belfry, and interior of the single-story, one-room structure were repaired and restored. A second major preservation effort took place 28 years later.

Backtrack east on Lake Street to Mineral Well Park, then continue east on the south side of Lake up to and across US-31 toward the Gaslight Shopping District, a historic concentration of stores that have continuously catered to resorters and visitors for more than a century. (For more details on walking the area's specialty shops and galleries, see pgs. 101-106.)

The first buildings here were wood structures built in the 1870s. Almost all — after burning or being torn down — were soon replaced by Victorian-era brick buildings. Queen Anne and Italianate styles dominate, with both borrowing and combining elements from previous architectural styles to achieve a high degree of ornamentation. Building fronts feature bracketed cornices, dentils (small, closely spaced, decorative rectangular blocks beneath cornices), window hoods, supporting lug sills and lintels, decorative slip sills, and capital-capped pilasters (false columns).

Having always been commercial buildings, the street levels are lined with lots of windows that both illuminate and allow good looks into retail areas. Upper stories originally housed (and still do, in many instances) offices and residences. Several of the mostly two- and three-story structures have been painted with multiple colors to emphasize sometimes-intricate, sometimes-elaborate architectural details.

From US-31 and Lake, go one block east on the south side of Lake to Petoskey Street. As you do, in view across Lake to the left (north) in the next block are 3½-foot-high, fading block letters that spell out "Petoskey Normal Business College" across the entire third-level west wall of the G & A Building (5). The college preparatory and teacher-training school opened in 1888 and operated out of several different Mitchell Street locations before moving here after the building was constructed in

1907. The school occupied the upper floors above a street-level souvenir bazaar operated by local Armenian families.

Cross Petoskey Street, continuing east on the south side of Lake. Across Lake adjoining the G & A Building on the east is J. W. Shorter Mercantile (311 E. Lake, built 1881) (6), whose second-level exterior is faced with beautifully designed pressed sheet metal, similar to more-familiar tin ceilings.

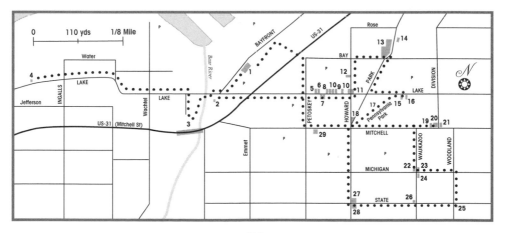

On the south side of Lake here, Items and In The Woods (7), at 316 and 318 E. Lake, each occupy a half of one of the city's few remaining first-generation, wood commercial structures. The Wild West-looking, false-fronted building, constructed in 1881, originally housed the National Hotel.

North across Lake from In the Woods, the second story of the G and O Building (8) — above Harbor Wear, at 319 E. Lake — is constructed of red Jacobsville (Keweenaw Peninsula) sandstone, which was popular and easy to get at the time of construction.

Protruding from the second-level brick wall above Bear Cub Kid-Fitters (325 E. Lake) is a vintage, green-and-white, metal, multi glass-bulbed "Hollywood" sign (9), a remnant from one of three movie theatres that once simultaneously operated in the city.

To its left (west) and right (east), the front roof edges of the buildings that house Windemere Clothiers, Apron Strings, and Cutlers (10) are all trimmed with pressed-metal cornices.

East across Howard Street from Cutlers, at the northeast corner of Lake and Howard, is Petoskey's first commercial brick building (11), constructed in 1879 to house the Central Drug Store where, 40 years later, Ernest Hemingway — during his stay in Petoskey p. 113) — is said to have regularly ordered malteds. The building now houses Symons General Store.

Turn left (north) along the west side of Howard and go about a half block to a two-story white-brick building (12) now occupied by Gattles linens and apparel but which 80 years ago housed Braun's Diner. Because the rooming house where Ernest Hemingway stayed did not serve meals, the author often ate at Braun's, which he later called "Browns Beanery" and described in his novel *Torrents of Spring*.

Follow Howard north (toward the bay) another half block to Bay Street. Turn right (east) along Bay and go one block to the large, cream-colored, porch-fronted Perry Hotel (13), which overlooks the bay from the northwest corner of Bay and Lewis. The hotel was built in 1899 by Norman J. Perry, a Petoskey dentist who had given up his practice after a female patient died in his office. The Perry is the city's first brick hotel, the reason in great part that it is also the only one remaining of Petoskey's more than 20 turn-of-the-century hotels.

East across Lewis, Penn Plaza professional offices occupy a former railroad station (14) constructed at the turn of the century on the site of the city's first train depot, built in 1875 and then destroyed by fire in 1899.

From the corner of Bay and Lewis, cross (south) Bay and follow Park Avenue, a sidewalk that angles southwest a block to Lake Street. Turn left (east) and follow Lake up a block to the City Park Grill (15). Two doors east on Lake is the Penn-Dixie office building (circa 1880s) (16), which architects say is a good example of the Richardsonian Romanesque style, characterized by the arched windows and "rusticated sandstone" surface.

The City Park Grill began life in 1875 as (Alanso) McCarthy's Hall, a male-only saloon/billiard room that was also the town's cultural and social center, in large part because it was one of few public places heated during the winter. Dances, the city's first theatre performances, governmental meetings, and even church services were held in a large upstairs hall with its own separate entrance.

A few years after opening, the establishment began providing food to guests at the Cushman Hotel, which once stood immediately west. Also, an outdoor dining/entertainment area called the Palm Garden — centered by a fountain and decorated with live Florida palms — was opened immediately east.

In 1910 new owners expanded further by opening the Grill Cafe east of the Palm Garden in the (current) Penn-Dixie Build-

ing. At about the same time, during a period of locally imposed prohibition, secret underground alcohol-delivery tunnels were constructed to connect all the buildings, including the hotel.

In the years since, the establishment has undergone several structural, ownership, and name changes. Surviving the remodelings and still dominating the interior of the City Park Grill are a vintage pressed-tin ceiling and a hand-carved walnut, cherry, and hickory bar, both installed before the turn of the century. The bar, according to local lore, was regularly elbowed by Ernest Hemingway during his time in the city.

Spreading south from the west side of the City Park Grill is tree-shaded, grassy Pennsylvania Park (17), which for several decades was a bustling railroad hub. Railroads not only contributed to Petoskey's early growth, they also helped define the area. The first train reached here in 1873 carrying a journalist who reported the area's unmatched natural beauty to downstaters. Almost instantly Petoskey — a then-crude shanty settlement with only a 100 or so non-Indian residents — became a proverbial tourist mecca.

For the next several years, Petoskey was the end of the line, with so-called "dummy trains" running regular shuttles to Harbor Springs, Bay View, and other "outlying" resort areas. At that time, counting everything that moved on rails, up to 90 trains chugged in and out of the city daily. And by the turn of the century, as many as 13,000 trains pulled into the city each year, dropping off tens of thousands of passengers who dispersed to more than 20 resort hotels — many elegant — that surrounded this park, which was then lined with five sets of tracks.

Not long after World War I, however,

passenger rail service declined proportionate to the growth of automobile travel and finally ended in the early 1960s.

Make your way to the southwest corner of the park and walk (west) out to Howard Street behind the Chamber of Commerce building, past newspaper vending machines and public telephones and restrooms. There only feet to the right (north) is the prow of the Flatiron Building (18), which is shaped like the now-antique, triangular household appliance with the same name. The Flatiron as well as Meyer Hardware (east across Pennsylvania Park), Penneys (south across Mitchell Street), and many other buildings throughout the city were constructed in their distinct angular shapes to accommodate the railroads' right of way.

Go north on Howard a few yards to Mitchell, turn left (east), and follow the

north side of Mitchell two blocks east to the Petoskey Public Library (19), on the left at 451 E. Mitchell. The small brick structure, opened in 1910, is a classic example of the more than 2,500 such facilities founded and/or funded by wealthy industrialist Andrew Carnegie.

Next door (and now connected) to the east is the Crooked Tree Arts Center (p. 103) (20), which occupies a preserved and partially restored, three-story, wood Gothic Revival Methodist church built in 1890.

East across Division Street, on the northeast corner of Division and Mitchell at 501 E. Mitchell, is the First Presbyterian Church (21). Presbyterian presence in Petoskey dates to 1852, when a church-sponsored mission and school were opened in the area (p. 118). The original church at this corner was constructed in 1888 as a Victorian-style wood building with a tall bell tower. During the centennial of the mission's founding, the church was remodeled to its current brick American Colonial style. In 1982 a second remodeling project returned the sanctuary to a Victorian look.

Backtrack west along Mitchell to just west of the library and cross Mitchell (south) on the marked crosswalk (vehicles are supposed to stop for pedestrians, but don't count on it) to Waukazoo Avenue. Go south along Waukazoo one block to Michigan Street. On the northwest corner there is a Christian Science Church (22), built in 1966 as a replacement for the group's original house of worship, which had stood there since 1911.

East across the street on the northeast corner of Waukazoo and Michigan is Temple B'Nai Israel (23). A synagogue has stood here since 1911, when the local (then-named) Ben Israel Congregation purchased and moved a small, 10-year-old, wood Baptist church from (south) across the street. Over the years the structure was enlarged and in 1975 was completely remodeled.

At the southeast corner of Waukazoo and Michigan is the large, brick First Baptist Church (24), built in 1911 after the group's original church was sold to and moved by the Ben Israel Congregation.

Head east on Michigan one block to Woodland Avenue, turn right (south), and go one block along Woodland to State Street. On the southeast corner of State and Woodland, at 602 State, is the former Eva Potter rooming house (25), where Ernest Hemingway lived during the fall and winter of 1919-1920 while recuperating from wounds received during service as a Red Cross ambulance driver during World War I. Twenty-year-old Hemingway launched his writing career from here, sending out his first stories (which were rejected) and working hard to perfect his craft. He also partied hard and wandered the city collecting characters, settings, and other materials that would later appear in his Nick Adams short stories and *The Torrents of Spring* and other novels.

Head west along State one block to Waukazoo Avenue. On the northwest corner of Waukazoo and State (514 Waukazoo) is the city's only known Sears, Roebuck and Co. mail-order kit home. (26) From 1908 to 1940 the catalog giant offered more than 450 different styles of the country's first prefabricated, mass-produced homes that 100,000 buyers ordered by mail. Sears offered this orange-brick, English cottage — called the Belmont — for only two years, 1932 and 1933. Ordered by the Jessie Baker (of the city's former Baker Shoes store) family in 1933 at a cost of $2,600, the house arrived in two railroad boxcars holding 30,000 pieces — right down to the last stud, rafter, screw, nail, light switch and doorknob. Local carpenters and craftsmen then used an accompanying 76-page instruction manual to put together the precut, notched, numbered, and otherwise-ready-to-assemble pieces.

Continue west along State one block to Howard Street. Dominating the northeast corner there — and in fact dominating the center-city area — is the 160-foot-long, 60-foot-wide St. Francis Xavier Catholic Church (27), whose slender steeple tops out at 168 feet above the street. Construction of the magnificent edifice began in 1903 and took five years to complete, with all labor and materials being donated. Local farmers hauled hand-cut fieldstone, elm timbers and rafters, sand, and gravel to the site in horse-drawn wagons. Bricks were made in Boyne City and shipped here by rail.

Inside, a high ceiling arches over a cavernous sanctuary softly illuminated by sev-

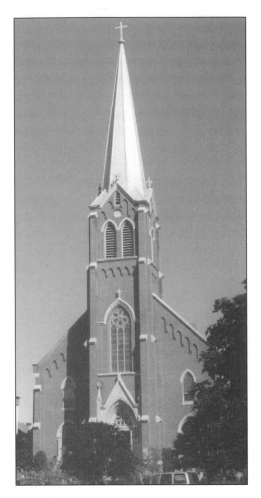

South across Mitchell there, at 316-318, is the Cook Building (29), built in the 1880s and currently housing Coldwell Banker Schmidt Realtors and Those Bloomin' Kids. Architects have described the building's elaborate second-level pressed-metal facade as the most dramatic in the city.

Continue west along Mitchell ¼ block to Petoskey Street, turn right (north), and go a block to Lake Street. From here return to the parking area by turning left (west) onto Lake and going 300 yards to Bayfront Drive and the museum. Or continue north along Petoskey Street one block to Bay Street, take the Bayfront Park tunnel under US-31 down to Bayfront Drive, turn left (west), and follow a blacktop sidewalk that winds between the base of a bluff and Bayfront Drive 125 yards to the museum.

eral stained-glass windows. Ornate features include a pulpit local artisans shaped from a single tree into a shell that naturally amplifies the priest's voice. (If you look inside, the church asks that you please use the State Street ramp to enter, not the front stairs.)

South across State Street is Central Elementary (28), the most recent in an evolution of public educational facilities that have occupied the site since 1875.

Walk north along Howard two blocks to Mitchell Street, cross Mitchell, then turn left (west) and follow Mitchell about ¾ block.

GREENWOOD CEMETERY

With nearly seven miles of narrow lanes winding through 90 acres of hilly, wooded, park-like grounds, Greenwood Cemetery is a uniquely beautiful place to walk.

This final destination can also be a most-interesting undertaking, a strangely fascinating connection with the area's past that books and museums can't provide. The 16,000 dead buried here all have tales to tell. Following are those of several dozen of Petoskey's most-notable, influential, interesting and colorful pioneers.

LOOP TRAIL ¾ MILE
ALLOW ONE HOUR

Facilities: None

Directions: From the junction of US-31 and US-131 go west on south US-31 0.2 miles to Greenwood (Cemetery) Road (at the west end of Fletch's auto dealership). Turn left (south) and go ¼ mile to the cemetery entrance, on the right (west). Park off the road near the cemetery headquarters, which is just a few yards in (west) from the entrance.

From in front of the headquarters building, walk west 25 yards to the first lane that branches off to the right (north). Turn right and go about 140 yards (crossing an east-west lane at about 90 yards) to a dead end at a cedar hedge. Turn left (west) and go 75 yards — with nice, elevated views of the bay along the way — to a 90-degree turn left (south).

On the left (east) just a few feet after making the turn is a modest, 3-ft high, 4-foot wide, gray, granite Pailthorp family marker (1). One of several foot-high headstones jutting up in front marks the plot of pioneer attorney, politician and judge Charles J. (C.J.) Pailthorp (1847-1948). Fresh out of the University of Michigan Law School, Pailthorp arrived in Petoskey — then little more than a shanty settlement — in the spring of 1875 and opened a law practice in offices above a grocery store. Prospective clients at the time numbered only 125 who were non-Ottawa Indians. One of Pailthorp's first actions was to help negotiate the sale of railroad-owned property to a Methodist association that used the land to begin what is now Bay View (pgs. 30-39).

In 1878 Pailthorp was elected to repre-

115

sent Antrim, Charlevoix, Otsego, and Emmet counties in the state legislature, and during his two-year term he was instrumental in securing official Village status for Petoskey. He also served as the area's Circuit Court Judge for two years, after which he returned to a long-time private practice, concluding his career at age 92 by arguing a case before the state supreme court.

Buried near C.J. Pailthorp and his wife, Jesse (1861-1936), is their daughter, Frances V. (1879-1968), a long-time Petoskey public-school art teacher who often recounted what a curiosity she, as the first red-haired baby born here, was to local Indians, who would peer at her through the windows of her family's home. Her brother Edwin G. "Dutch" Pailthorp (1900-1972) became good friends with Ernest Hemingway during the later-famous author's stay in Petoskey (p. 113).

Continue south 50 yards then curve gradually left (southeast) 60 yards (past a lane that branches off left) to a T junction. Turn right (south) and go 50 yards to another T junction. Turn right (west) and just a few steps farther, at the intersection of four lanes, take the second lane from the left (straight across), which rises and winds southwest about 60 yards to a fork.

Turn right (west) and immediately on the left is a large but plain, rectangular polished-granite Bump family marker (2). Included among eight 18-inch-high headstones is one for Lucy M. (Mrs. G. W.) Bump (1849-1929) who, from her arrival in 1875, owned Petoskey's first piano and was the area's first piano teacher. The long-time Methodist Church organist also owned the area's first portable organ, which she transported by wagon to play at social events.

Under the limbs of a large maple, just to the right of, slightly behind, and facing opposite (south) the Bump plot is a textured-granite Hampton family marker (3). One of the surrounding headstones marks the plot for Charles Sumner Hampton (1856-1917) who, in 1875 after graduating at age 19 from Adrian College, came here and organized 100 students into Petoskey's first bona fide school, with primary and upper departments. After spending only one year as principal in a new wooden schoolhouse on the southeast corner of Howard and State, Hampton moved to Little Traverse (now Harbor Springs) and started that settlement's first organized school.

The following year, at age 21, he was elected to the first of two terms as justice of the peace. In 1884 Hampton founded Emmet County's first daily newspaper, *The Daily Resorter,* which he both reported for and edited while also occasionally still teaching. Over the ensuing decades, the paper changed owners and names several times while evolving into the current *Petoskey News-Review*

Return to the asphalt lane and continue west about 10 yards to just a few feet before a road branches off left (southwest). There on the left (south) is a large Ramsdell family marker (4), and among several foot-high headstones is one for Oscar Luman (1863-1924), a physician who was the city's first automobile owner. In 1904 Ramsdell ordered a single-cylinder Cadillac — price, $950 — which was delivered by train and which he drove over wagon-rutted, often-muddy streets.

Continue west on the asphalt lane (past a road that branches off left, south) about 70 yards to a magnificent, monstrous birch — perhaps the Petoskey area's largest — on the right (north), just before reaching roads that converge at the north side of Cannon Park.

Directly left (south) across the road from the tree is a Wachtel family marker (5), whose engraving faces (south) away from the road and requires stepping around to the other side to see. A few feet in front (south) of the large stone are two simple headstones for Phillip B. (1851-1913) and his wife, Alice Salisbury Wachtel (1853-1931).

Phillip and his father, John, came here from Pennsylvania in 1878 and opened Emmet County's first real bank in a temporary Mitchell Street location. Having also a temporary monopoly, deposits were

high enough that the Wachtels soon moved to a new building at the northwest corner of Mitchell and Howard, which has remained a banking site to this day.

Phillip later went into real estate and insurance businesses and also over the years served variously as Bear Creek Township Supervisor, Petoskey Village President, and Petoskey City Mayor, Treasurer, and Assessor.

Return to the asphalt and continue west just a few yards to a five-way junction on the north side of Cannon Park. Turn onto the rightmost lane and head generally north, immediately crossing an east-west lane, then passing between a Redpath

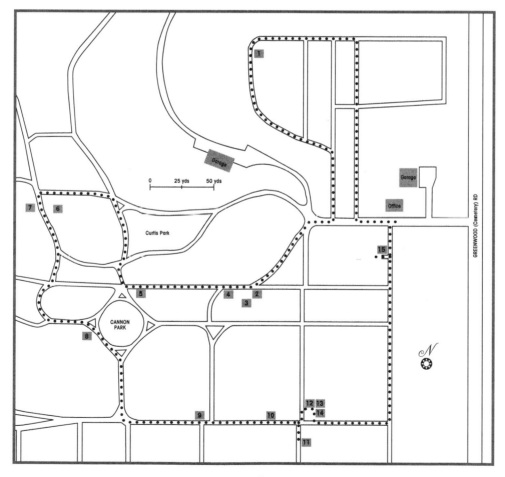

marker, on the left, and a few feet farther a magnificent European Beech, on the right (east). A few yards farther the lane reaches the intersection with another east-west lane. Turn left (west) and go about 60 yards to an intersection with a north-south lane.

Turn left (south), and about 10 yards farther about 25 feet off the lane to the left (east) is a Hill family marker (6). Four headstones include one for John G. Hill (1836-1911), Petoskey's first Village Attorney, who subsequently also served two terms as prosecuting attorney interrupted by a year spent as editor of the newspaper founded by Rozelle Rose (marker 13).

Directly (west) across the road, behind a small clump of cedars and under a maple, is a 6-inch-high headstone (7) for Rachel Oakley (1837-1910), Petoskey's first public-school teacher. When a Presbyterian mission and school, which had operated for more than 20 years closed in early 1874, a public school board organized and they hired Oakley, who had just arrived in the area. Beginning November 1874, Oakley intermittently conducted one-room classes in a small wood building for one school year. The next fall a "real" school opened in a new location under the direction of Charles S. Hampton (marker 3).

Return to the lane and continue south about 70 yards to a fork. Bear right (south) and go 15 yards to the intersection with an east-west lane. Cross the lane then wind 25 yards to a dead end at another east-west lane. Turn left (east) and head toward Cannon Park, bearing right (southeast) at about 25 yards at a fork around a large grassy triangle just before the park.

Across from the grassy triangle, just feet off the lane to the right (south) are a group of ten simple headstones, followed by a large stone memorial (8) to the Porters, Petoskey's first white family.

Andrew Porter (1817-1899) arrived here with his 75-year-old mother and his sister, Ann, on June 1, 1852, to establish a Presbyterian mission and school for the Bear River Band of Ottawa Indians. Porter soon married Mary G. (1822-1904) and expanded mission activities to include an 80-acre farm and a grist mill powered by the first dam placed on the Bear River.

By December 1857, an official Bear River post office was established, with Andrew its first postmaster. The facility consisted of a two drawers — one labeled "in," the other "out" — in a cabinet in the Porter home.

Porter's mother had come here planning to use her experience as a lay-doctor in their Pennsylvania home area. But — given the relatively primitive skills and knowledge of even educated physicians of the time — she didn't have the medical resources to save her first two grandchildren. In June 1855, Mary Porter gave birth to Lizzie Anne, who died six years later of whooping cough. A second child, born in the summer of 1857, lived only six weeks. Though named Joseph Glenn at birth, he is identified on his tombstone only as "baby Porter." In 1863 a son, Joseph Howard, was born; mother Porter died in 1867; and a little more than four years later Joseph, age eight, died of scarlet fever.

Just a couple of years later, the mission and school ran out of funds, and Andrew and Mary Porter went back to his Pennsylvania home. They returned not long after, however, to live out their remaining years near their only child to survive to adulthood, son Reuben, who practiced dentistry here.

Continue southeast 15 yards past another grass triangle then south about 40 yards to the intersection with an east-west lane.

Turn left (east) and follow the perfectly straight lane about 50 yards to just before the intersection of a north-south lane. There, on the left, is one of the cemetery's most unique and noticeable markers (9), for the McIntyre family. The natural, distinctively shaped and colored boulder was formed during the earth's molten beginnings and then, some 3-5 billion years later, carried here from Canada and dropped by Ice Age glaciers. Such "glacial erratics," as geologists term them, were often used by early settlers throughout the state as inexpensive tombstones. (photo, p. 121)

Continue straight (east), cross the intersection and go about 35 yards to the McManus family marker (10), a unique, layered piece of stonework topped by a 3-foot-diameter, polished-granite orb.

William L. McManus (1843-1922)

started Emmet County's first and most-successful lumber mill in 1876 along the Bear River within what is now the Petoskey city limits.

And though in his nearly 50 years here he made many civic contributions, including serving as mayor, he also was the plaintiff in the county's longest-running lawsuit, a riparian-rights dispute. In 1890 McManus purchased the land on both sides of the Bear River at its source, Bear (now Walloon) Lake, and replaced an existing dam with one wider and lower. As a result the lake level dropped, prompting lake property owners to sue. The litigation carried on for more than 20 years, with the cottagers and resort owners ultimately prevailing.

Continue east about 30 yards to the next intersection, turn right (south), and go about 15 yards to an old, weathered 6-foot-high marker (11) for Petoskey's first physician, Dr. William Little (1842-1875), and his family.

William and his brother Robert arrived here in the summer of 1873 after being recruited by businessman and experienced northern-Michigan frontier developer H.O. Rose (marker 11). In addition to running a medical practice, William partnered with his brother in the construction, begun in fall 1873, of the settlement's first bona fide hotel. That December, when Bear River was officially renamed, Dr. Little was appointed "Petoskey's" first postmaster. The post office plus Petoskey's first drug store, also run by the Littles, were located in their hotel, named the Rose House in honor of H.O. Rose. And after winning an 1875 election for Bear Creek Township Supervisor, one of William's first acts was to purchase the land and officially establish this cemetery.

Frequent bad-weather, winter "house-calls" by horseback far into the woods and across the bay — with occasional plunges through the ice — however, took their toll on the doctor's health. He died at age 33 only two years after arriving here, and was one of the first to be buried in the cemetery he had just created.

Backtrack north, cross the east-west lane, and go about 25 yards to a large, rough-granite Rose family marker (12) that faces north just off the road to the right (east). Among several nearby individual markers is a small, well-worn, ground-level gravestone for the man considered to be Petoskey's founding father, Hiram Obed Rose (1830-1911).

Prior to coming to Petoskey, Rose had successively set up businesses in the then-frontier settlements of Northport and Charlevoix. Rose's various enterprises thrived when railroads soon reached each town.

Rose arrived here in 1873, intent on using past experience and profits to turn what was basically an Indian settlement into a booming industrial and resort area. He purchased almost all of the city's present waterfront, including rocky bluffs he quarried for the manufacture of lime. In late fall 1873, just weeks before the first train arrived here, he completed a dock for a boat line that connected what was then the end of the rail line to Mackinac Island.

In the spring of 1875, Rose — with the help of lawyer C.J. Pailthorp (marker 1) — facilitated the sale of railroad-owned property to a Methodist association that used the land to begin what is now Bay View (pgs. 30-39).

Rose's business enterprises also variously included a general store, a hotel, and a sawmill. When Petoskey was officially in-corporated as a village in 1879, Rose was elected President, and he later helped establish the community's first public water system and first electric-power plant.

Directly east of and adjacent to the Rose plot is a marker (13) for the Jarmans, the third white family to settle in Petoskey. Though the father, Nathan (1841-1928), was Baptist, he was asked to come here in 1873 by Andrew Porter (marker 8) to help with the Methodist's struggling mission, school and farm. Within a year, Jarman rented the farm, allowing Porter and his wife to return to their Pennsylvania home. Jarman later bought the mission property and buildings and also ran the Antrim Lime Company, whose quarry was across Greenwood Road from this cemetery at the current site of Bay Mall. Nathan also became a real estate agent, served as a city councilman, and was active in the Baptist church.

Just a few feet south from the end of the line of Jarman headstones is an inconspicuous ground-level gravestone (14) for Rozelle Rose (1847-1908). Though also located just a few feet away from the Hiram Rose plot and though Rozelle was a contemporary of Hiram's, they were not related.

In 1875 Rozelle Rose wrote, edited, and published the *Emmet County Democrat*, Petoskey's first continuous newspaper. A year's subscription for the weekly cost $1.50, and Rose sometimes accepted payment in firewood, which he stored outside the newspaper office. When Rose noticed that some townspeople were helping themselves to his wood, he warned in the *Democrat*, "We (are thinking) strongly of putting some powder in a few sticks, and then somebody's dinner will make a map of some foreign country on the ceiling above the stove."

Rose could not make a consistent financial go of the paper, however, and during the winter of 1886 sold it at a loss. Over the ensuing years the *Democrat's* name and owners changed several times, ultimately being combined with two other papers into a single newspaper that was the forerunner of today's *Petoskey News-Review*.

From the Rozelle Rose gravestone, walk across the grass back (south) about 10 feet to the east-west road, turn left (east), and go 50 yards to where it makes a 90-degree turn left (north). On the left (north) just before the road curves, is a fine horse-chestnut tree specimen.

Follow the lane north about 125 yards to a short asphalt parking pad that branches off left (west), just before the headquarters building. Just north of the pad a 4-foot-diameter boulder (15) memorializes the man for whom the city of Petoskey is named, Ignatius Pe-to-se-ga (circa 1787-1884).

Pe-to-se-ga's mother, an Ottawa, was married to a fur trader who worked at Mackinac Island. As a result, Pe-to-se-learned the English language and European business practices and became a successful fur trader, hunter, fisherman and merchant.

He and his wife, Kes-way-gah (circa 1795 - 1881), settled at Little Traverse (now Harbor Springs), where they joined the Catholic Church, were baptized, and given the Christian names Ignatius and Mary. They had ten children, the three eldest of whom, when the time came, Ignatius insisted on sending out of state to be educated at Protestant colleges. Mary, a devout Catholic, disagreed so strongly that the couple separated. Ignatius and the children moved to the south side of the bay,

and Mary stayed at Little Traverse until a Catholic mission was built at Bear River (Petoskey) in 1859.

During the 1850s, through treaties and purchases, Pe-to-se-ga and his children acquired most of the land on which the city now stands, and so when whites began moving into the area, they respectfully referred to Ignatius as "chief," and the honorary title stuck.

And in late 1873 when pioneers needed to select a name for the village they were platting, they decided to further honor the then 87-year-old chief. Because the Ottawa had no written language, English-speaking writers spelled the Indians' words and names phonetically, with spelling for the same words often varying from writer to writer. As a result, Ignatius' last name had been variously written "Petawsegay," "Petosega" and — what was settled upon as the village's name — "Petoskey," Ottawa for "rising sun."

ABOUT THE AUTHOR

Gary W. Barfknecht, 56, was born and raised in Virginia, Minnesota, the "Queen City" of that state's Mesabi Iron Range. After receiving a bachelor of science degree from the University of Minnesota in 1967 and a master of science degree from the University of Washington in 1969, he came to Flint, Michigan, as a paint chemist with the E.I. DuPont & deNemours Company.

But after only a year on the job, Barfknecht and the chemical giant reached the mutual conclusion that he was not suited for corporate life, and Barfknecht set out on a freelance writing career. He sold the first magazine article he ever wrote, "Robots Join the Assembly Line" (*Science & Mechanics*, October 1971), and over the next few years, his articles were featured in *Reader's Digest, Science Digest, Lion, Sign, Lutheran Standard, Modern Maturity* and other magazines. He also was the ghost writer for the book, *A Father, A Son, and a Three Mile Run* (Zondervan, 1974) and authored and self-published a local guide book, *33 Hikes From Flint* (Friede Publications, 1975).

While freelancing, Barfknecht also managed a hockey pro shop at Flint's I.M.A. ice arena. In 1977 he suspended his writing efforts when he became director of almost all amateur hockey programming in the Genesee County area.

In 1981 he resigned as hockey commissioner to again become a fulltime author and publisher, and a year later he self-published what became a best-selling collection of Michigan trivia titled *Michillaneous*. Barfknecht followed with six other Michigan books: *Murder, Michigan* (1983), *Mich-Again's Day* (1984), *Michillaneous II* (1985), *Ultimate Michigan Adventures* (1989), *Unexplained Michigan Mysteries* (1993), and *The Michigan Book of Bests* (2000).

As owner and Managing Editor of Friede Publications, Barfknecht has brought 17 books into print by other Michigan authors, including *A Traveler's Guide to 116 Michigan Lighthouses* and *A Guide to 199 Michigan Waterfalls* by the Penrose family, *Natural Michigan* and *Michigan State and National Parks: A Complete Guide* by Tom Powers, *Canoeing Michigan Rivers* by Jerry Dennis, and a six-volume Michigan fishing guide series by Tom Huggler.

After living in Davison for 27 years, Barfknecht and his wife, Ann, relocated to Petoskey in 1999.

Daughter Heidi is an educator in Arlington, Virginia.

In Atlanta, daughter Amy and her husband, Dan, take good care of their son Anders, 3, and daughter Ella, 2, between visits from grandma and grandpa.